Sherman's March
through North Carolina

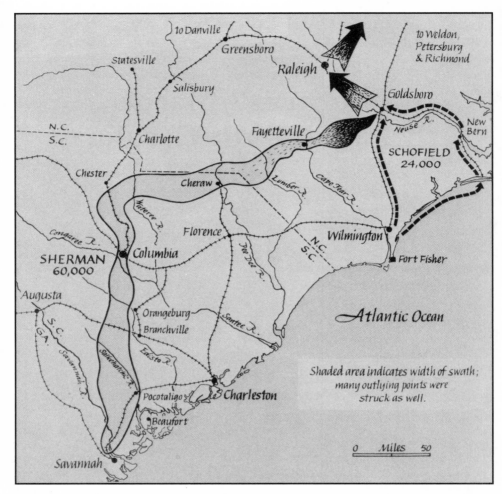

This map shows the route taken by Union forces under the command of Maj. Gen. William T. Sherman in the spring of 1865. Sherman's troops entered North Carolina from near Cheraw, South Carolina, on March 7 and departed the state north of Warrenton on May 4, entering Virginia. Map from Shelby Foote, *The Civil War: A Narrative. Red River to Appomattox* (New York: Random House, 1974), 752; reproduced by permission.

Sherman's March through North Carolina

A Chronology

Wilson Angley   Jerry L. Cross   Michael Hill

Raleigh
Division of Archives and History
North Carolina Department of Cultural Resources

**North Carolina Division of Archives and History
Research Branch**

Jerry C. Cashion, *Supervisor*
Ph.D., University of North Carolina at Chapel Hill

Wilson Angley, *Researcher*
Ph.D., University of North Carolina at Chapel Hill

Jerry L. Cross, *Researcher*
Ph.D., State University of New York at Binghamton

Michael Hill, *Researcher*
M.A., University of North Carolina at Chapel Hill

The Research Branch wishes to express its gratitude to Miss Lisa Kay Keenum, branch secretary, who went well beyond the call of duty to see this report completed.

Contents

Maps

Foreword

On May 26, 1994, the North Carolina Historical Commission considered a proposal from the Cape Fear Living History Society to place a monument at Bentonville Battleground State Historic Site. The monument would recognize and commemorate those Union troops who fought and died in the largest Civil War battle in North Carolina, the Battle of Bentonville, in March 1865. The monument would be paid for by private subscription and would contain the names of the Union corps present. No names of individuals (including that of William T. Sherman) nor any depiction of any person was proposed for the monument.

Nearly three weeks before the meeting the Raleigh *News and Observer* published a letter from a concerned citizen implying that the proposed monument would be a statue of General Sherman and would be paid for by the state. All hell broke loose. Hundreds of phone calls, letters, and petitions, mostly in opposition to any monument, came pouring in.

At the meeting on May 26, the commission voted to defer consideration of the monument until November and instructed me to report at that time on the operations of Sherman's forces in North Carolina from the time they entered the state until the time they departed. On June 16 I directed Dr. Jerry C. Cashion, head of the Division of Archives and History's Research Branch, to undertake the study that follows. Over our long association, starting from my first day as a graduate student in history at UNC-Chapel Hill in 1967, I had known Jerry Cashion to be an indefatigable researcher who would pursue historical accuracy wherever it might lead. Anyone who reads the work produced here by Dr. Cashion and his fine staff will be impressed by its accuracy and thoroughness.

Dr. Cashion's report was completed on September 30, 1994, weeks in advance of the commission's November 3 meeting date. When the commission met, Dr. H. G. Jones moved for approval of the monument. After considerable discussion, the commission defeated Jones's proposal by a vote of six to five.

Regardless of that vote or what future proposals there may be at Bentonville or elsewhere, *Sherman's March through North Carolina: A Chronology* stands as a remarkable account of a remarkable time. If the whole furor swirling around the proposed Union monument at Bentonville produced "much heat and little light," what follows is illumination.

William S. Price Jr., *Former Director*
Division of Archives and History

June 1996

Introduction

"War is cruelty and you cannot refine it," William Tecumseh Sherman informed the mayor of Atlanta after he ordered the expulsion of the occupied city's civilian population. During the ensuing months Sherman would act upon that dictum with a grim determination and remorseless fury that left a smoldering swath of destruction and ruin in its wake. If, as some military historians have suggested, Sherman was one of the first proponents of modern warfare, then the South—more particularly Georgia and the Carolinas—suffered the consequences of total war. Sherman's march, for Southerners and Northerners alike, passed into legend. But as in so many other legends, it had a firm basis in fact.

Having taken Atlanta in September 1864, Sherman grew impatient with the inconclusive skirmishing between his army and Confederate forces under John Bell Hood. Sherman longed to break out. He proposed to Ulysses S. Grant that he "divide the Confederacy in two, and come up on the rear of [Robert E.] Lee" by marching to the sea. At first Grant hesitated. To disengage with Hood and abandon supply lines in the midst of hostile territory was a dangerous gamble. Sherman insisted that his battle-hardened troops, numbering more than sixty thousand, would find plenty to eat in the countryside "and make Georgia howl" in the process. Grant relented. On November 15, 1864, Sherman's army burned everything of ostensible military value (and then some) in Atlanta and began its march to the sea. In deciding to live off the land, Sherman, intentionally or not, gave license to unscrupulous and undisciplined troops to commit excesses. In the 285 miles between Atlanta and Savannah, Sherman faced only token opposition. According to one Union officer, the march became "the most gigantic pleasure excursion ever planned."

For Georgians along the sixty-mile-wide corridor that Sherman's army scoured, the march was anything but a picnic. Foraging soldiers, known as "bummers," stripped farms, plantations, and even slave quarters of food, valuables, and livestock. What the bluecoats could not carry or consume on the spot they destroyed. In targeting civilians Sherman sought to cripple the South's capacity to make war by denying its soldiers supplies and breaking the will of the Southern people. Compounding Georgians' misery were the depredations of Confederate stragglers and cavalrymen under Joseph Wheeler. After mid-1864, Wheeler's horsemen, like Sherman's army, had to live off the land. The Confederate troops showed no more compunction than Sherman's men in stealing and plundering. Georgia unionists and newly liberated slaves also joined in the pillaging. Five weeks after leaving Atlanta, Sherman entered Savannah. As a Christmas gift, Sherman presented the city to Abraham Lincoln.

Sherman now turned his unyielding attention to South Carolina. Sherman and Grant wanted to crush Lee's Army of Northern Virginia in a giant vise formed by their two armies. To close that vise, Union forces would have to drive north from Savannah through the interior of the Carolinas, destroying the resources of war as they went. Sherman welcomed the opportunity. His soldiers, he candidly admitted, wanted to punish the state that had incited the rebellion. "[T]he whole army," said Sherman, "is burning with an insatiable desire to wreak vengeance upon South Carolina. I almost tremble at her fate, but feel that she deserves all that seems to be in store for her." One of his soldiers proclaimed: "Here is where treason began and, by God, here is where it shall end!" On February 1, 1865, Sherman set his troops in motion toward the heart of secessionism.

The path that Sherman's army cut through South Carolina was narrower than that through Georgia, but the level of destruction was more intense. With the exception of Atlanta, relatively few houses in Georgia were burned. In South Carolina few escaped the torch. Arson reached a pinnacle at Columbia on the night of February 17–18. Retreating Confederate forces, drunken Union soldiers, Union prisoners from a nearby prison camp, local criminals who had fled jail, liberated slaves, and gale-force winds combined to create a conflagration that consumed one-third of the city. Sherman may not have started the fire, but he and his troops helped extinguish it.

Sherman later labeled the march to the sea in Georgia "child's play" compared to the Carolinas campaign. Constant rain and swampy terrain impeded the bluecoats' progress through the lower portions of South Carolina. Wheeler's cavalry harassed Union forces as they tried to cross rain-swollen rivers and streams. To negotiate routes that were literally under water, Sherman employed soldiers and liberated slaves to cut trees for "corduroy" roads, to erect bridges, and to build causeways. The sheer engineering feat of Sherman's march awed even his Confederate adversaries. William J. Hardee and Joseph E. Johnston expressed disbelief at Sherman's steady rate of twelve miles per day. Johnston compared Sherman's accomplishments to those of Julius Caesar.

By the end of February, Sherman was poised to enter North Carolina. Would he order a surcease to the indiscriminate foraging, pillaging, and arson that had left a smoking hell in South Carolina? Not everyone in Sherman's army embraced the total-war philosophy. Some officers had adopted stern measures to control the orgy of destruction but with little effect. North Carolina had been the last state to secede, and it harbored many unionists as well as the largest peace movement in the Confederacy. Would Sherman and his men treat the Old North State with the same brutality directed at Georgia and South Carolina? North Carolinians fearfully turned their eyes to the south. In the following pages the Research Branch of the Division of Archives and History offers a thorough and compelling chronology of Sherman's march in North Carolina.

Jeffrey J. Crow, *Director*
Division of Archives and History

June 1996

PART 1

March 1–March 14, 1865

March 1 (Wednesday)

In its lead editorial of this date, the *North Carolina Standard* of Raleigh expressed grave concern regarding the steady approach of Gen. William T. Sherman's army of sixty thousand men. That veteran force, deployed in two wings, with cavalry accompaniment, had moved northward from Savannah through the very heartlands of Georgia and South Carolina. The right wing (Army of the Tennessee), under the command of Gen. Oliver O. Howard, consisted of Gen. John A. Logan's Fifteenth Corps and Gen. Frank P. Blair Jr.'s Seventeenth Corps. The left wing (Army of Georgia), commanded by Gen. Henry W. Slocum, was comprised of the Fourteenth and Twentieth Corps, led by Gen. Jefferson C. Davis and Gen. Alpheus S. Williams respectively. Reporting directly to Sherman was Gen. Judson Kilpatrick, whose cavalry division followed a route generally to the west and north of the army's main columns.[1] The owner and editor of the *North Carolina Standard*, William W. Holden, had run unsuccessfully for governor during the previous year, and for many months he had fanned the spreading flames of war-weariness and disaffection in the state. Holden's editorial expressed not only concern but also a widespread and agonizing uncertainty as to where Sherman's path through North Carolina might lead:

> The latest news may be given in a few words—Charleston, Wilmington, and Columbia are in the hands of the enemy, and Sherman is supposed to be moving in heavy force on Chesterville [Chester], which is some forty-five miles south of Charlotte. It seems to be understood that the Confederate forces will make a stand at Chesterville. We hope for the best, but we confess we fear that Sherman will not be routed, or even checked. It may also turn out that columns of the enemy are preparing to advance through the State on a line considerably to the east of Charlotte. Goldsborough, Fayetteville, and even Raleigh are in danger. We fear that what has been will be; in other words, that the enemy will overrun this country. . . .
> The prospect is gloomy. We can see no blessed star pointing to peace, but on every side the clouds of war. How many more widows and orphans, how much more suffering,

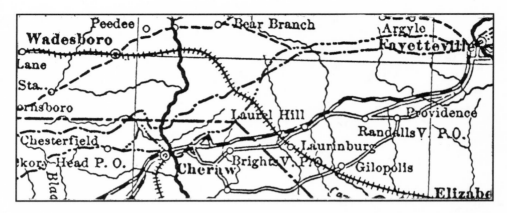

Troops under Sherman's command traversed these areas of South Carolina and North Carolina between March 1 and March 14, 1865. Detail of map from Manning F. Force, *General Sherman* (New York: D. Appleton and Company, 1899), opposite 295.

and how many more of the true and brave of our veteran troops must be slaughtered before the end shall come.[2]

Holden could scarcely have known, as he wrote, that the first of Sherman's troops would enter North Carolina on the very day his editorial appeared.

Sherman, in fact, was approaching the South Carolina town of Chesterfield from the west on this day, having passed well to the south of his supposed objective, Chester. He would reach Chesterfield on the following day, traveling with the Twentieth Corps of the left wing.[3] Beyond Chesterfield lay Cheraw, toward which Confederate forces under Gen. William J. Hardee were hastening from Charleston. As Gen. Joseph E. Johnston himself viewed the situation, "It was a question, on the 1st of March, whether the troops of the department, coming from Charleston, or the Federal army, would reach Cheraw first."[4]

Sherman's cavalry troops were moving eastward on a line slightly north of both the Fourteenth and Twentieth Corps. It was probably an advance detachment of Kilpatrick's horsemen that crossed the North Carolina line into Union County on this day, although far-ranging foragers from the left wing may have accomplished this initial entry into the state. In any event, this first of many raids to come was directed at Monroe, the county seat. Hardest hit during this brief foray was a group of hapless refugees from South Carolina. The *Western Democrat* of Charlotte carried the following account of the incident in its issue of March 7:

> On Wednesday last about 3 o'clock, a squad of thirty-five Yankee cavalry slashed into the village of Monroe, Union County, remained about an hour and left, carrying off all the horses and mules they could gather up. A train of wagons, ten in number, belonging to a party of refugees from Chester District had just reached the village and were standing in the street when the Yankees appeared. Of course the train was seized, and horses, mules, and wagons with their contents, and 19 negro men were carried off. . . . The loss is a heavy one for the unfortunate refugees, for we suppose the wagons contained all the valuables they possessed. The women and children that accompanied the wagons were left standing in the streets of Monroe.

No buildings were burnt in the village—not even the Court House and jail were injured—but the enemy seized whatever they wanted and carried it off. Two couriers (sent out from this place) stationed at Monroe, were captured. . . .[5]

Several days after the raid on Monroe, a local resident wrote to the editor of the *Western Democrat*, identifying the Union horsemen as "a squad of Kilpatrick's robbers" and alleging that he and his family had been robbed at gunpoint: "I had two carbines presented by them at my bosom at one time. They presented their guns at the breast of my innocent wife and defenceless daughter, demanding gold and silver, threatened to shoot us and burn our house. They got my wife's gold watch. . . . Mr. Editor, is this the way to coax us back into the Union?"[6]

As it happened, the *Western Democrat* had another incident of March 1 to report—in this case involving turncoat Southerners who had been apprehended by Confederate troops in the Charlotte area. Four "galvanized Yankees" were executed by their captors on this date "for the crime of desertion." Two others would be shot less than a week later.[7]

Meanwhile, in the state capital, Treasurer Jonathan Worth and Gov. Zebulon B. Vance had been agonizing over the increasingly serious problem of Confederate deserters, particularly in Randolph County. In a lengthy letter to a brother in that county, Worth set forth some rather drastic but carefully considered proposals to alleviate conditions there:

> You describe the deserters in Randolph under two classes—the one concealing themselves and thus avoiding the field [military service], from the want of courage or religious scruples. . . . The other class consisting of lawless desperadoes who rob promiscuously and occasionally commit murder and other outrages to justify malignant feeling or get money. . . .
>
> I entertain no doubt, owing to the terrible state of things in the County, but that the Govr. will readily assent to the Home Guards staying at home, upon conditions that they immediately organise, elect officers and go immediately to work in real earnest to capture or expel the vicious deserters.[8]

On this same day Governor Vance added his endorsement to Worth's letter, while making it clear that the citizens of Randolph "must show a disposition to help themselves" and that "No half way business" would be tolerated.[9]

March 2 (Thursday)

Sherman and sizable elements of the Twentieth Corps entered the village of Chesterfield, South Carolina, the leading division having skirmished briefly with Confederate cavalrymen under Gen. Matthew C. Butler. The Fourteenth Corps followed a parallel course, slightly to the north, as Kilpatrick's cavalry began moving into North Carolina in considerable force. While in Chesterfield Sherman received word that the Fifteenth and Seventeenth Corps had moved eastward nearly to Cheraw. Within Cheraw itself, Hardee was assembling his weary forces as they arrived from the coast.[10] Meanwhile, Gen. P. G. T. Beauregard was taking steps to regulate the impressment of farm animals by Confederate troops in the Charlotte area. The *Western Democrat* heartily welcomed this overdue restraint on the "wholesale impressment" of recent times but expressed concern that the practice was already so widespread that "some of our farmers will not be able to make a crop for the want of horses and mules."[11] The paper also noted that "orders have been sent out to shoot any one seizing horses who has not the proper authority to impress." "We think it probable," the journal continued, "that many of those who profess to have authority to take horses and mules are nothing but rogues."[12]

During the afternoon a contingent of Capt. George A. Smith's company of the Anson County Home Guard hastened to the southern portion of that county "to operate against a small foraging party that were committing depredations in that section." Among the members of Smith's unit was Frank Darley, editor and publisher of the *Argus* of Wadesboro. At Maysville those Home Guardsmen and others observed firsthand some of the destruction accomplished by the foragers, including a burned dwelling house and outbuildings on at least one plantation.[13] In the days to follow, Sherman's men would make their presence felt in Wadesboro and throughout Anson County.

In nearby Randolph County, to the north, the depredations of Confederate deserters continued unabated. During the evening hours a large band of those deserters entered the home of Mrs. I. H. Foust, a widow, breaking open a safe and stealing valuables and provisions after locking Mrs. Foust and her daughter in an adjoining room. An Asheboro resident complained to Jonathan Worth that such acts were "becoming a daily occurrence."[14]

March 3 (Friday)

Traveling eastward with the Twentieth Corps through a drizzling rain, Sherman entered Cheraw approximately two hours after leaving Chesterfield. Brief skirmishes with Butler's cavalry occurred along the way. The Fifteenth and Seventeenth Corps moved a shorter distance into town from their encampments of the previous night. The Fourteenth Corps, meanwhile, was en route to Sneedsborough, with directions to cross the Pee Dee River at that point. As the first Federal units entered Cheraw, Hardee's Confederate troops crossed over the Pee Dee after lively skirmishing, taking care to destroy the bridge behind them. Once safely across, Hardee directed his troops northward toward Greensboro, in accordance with his most recent orders.[15]

Hardee's hasty evacuation of Cheraw left behind vast quantities of munitions and supplies that had been transported northward from Charleston. Such items as could not be readily used by Sherman's forces were destroyed, together with railroad facilities and bridges as far southward as Darlington.[16]

It was while at Cheraw that Sherman was exasperated to find that the *New York Tribune* had publicized the fact that Goldsboro was his North Carolina objective. This, not surprisingly, he "thought extremely mischievous": "Up to that moment I had endeavored so to feign to our left that we had completely misled our antagonists; but this was no longer possible, and I concluded that we must be ready for the concentration in our front of all the force subject to Jos. Johnston's orders. . . ."[17]

It was also in Cheraw that Sherman learned that Gen. Joseph E. Johnston was slated to replace Gen. P. G. T. Beauregard as commander of all Confederate forces in the two Carolinas. The significance of that change of command was clearly not lost on Sherman; nor would it be lost on other high-ranking Federal officers or on the thousands of enlisted men under them. Their new opponent would almost certainly prove far more resourceful and formidable.[18]

This day brought the first of two major Union cavalry raids on Wadesboro and widespread despoliation throughout Anson County as a whole. As it happened, one eyewitness to the occurrences in Wadesboro was the Episcopal bishop of North Carolina, Thomas Atkinson, who at the time was residing with his family in the community. One of Judson Kilpatrick's troopers robbed Atkinson at gunpoint in the bishop's own home, then proceeded to ransack the house for valuables. Similar incidents, according to Atkinson, took place in "every house in town where there seemed to be anything worth taking."[19] Indeed, for several days it was widely and falsely reported that "the village of Wadesboro" had not only been pillaged but also "burnt" by Kilpatrick's horsemen.[20]

The hapless editor of the Wadesboro *Argus* had the misfortune to return to town with his Home Guard unit just as the raid commenced, having endeavored since the previous day to prevent depredations in outlying areas:

We rode leisurely on back, and had just reached the Court House, where we found a motley crowd of Home Guard, aged citizens, children and negroes, many of them much frightened at a report that the whole of Kilpatrick's command was advancing on the town, and we had just dismounted, when a body of the enemy—some seventy-five or a hundred in number— were seen rising the hill by the Masonic Hall and dashing towards the Court House, yelling and firing at the crowd in front of that building. There were not more than ten of us who had arms in our hands and when the enemy were first seen they could not have been more than a hundred yards from us. A stampede instantly took place by the crowd, and we found ourself standing alone in the middle of the street, bullets whizzing all around us. . . . The party, after dispersing the crowd assembled in front of the Court House, soon spread through the principal streets arresting and robbing them of their hats, boots, watches and pocket-books, and stealing all the mules they could lay their hands upon.[21]

Darley, in fact, was one of approximately three dozen Wadesboro citizens who suffered the double misfortune of being both robbed and taken prisoner by the Union soldiers. He was not released until a week later, following the Battle of Monroe's Crossroads.[22]

Even Darley, however, acknowledged later that the depredations in Wadesboro "were comparatively light [compared to] what they were in the lower portion of the county, where the main body of the [Union] cavalry were operating."[23] There, numerous farmers and planters saw their homes and outbuildings ransacked, crops and provisions destroyed, livestock taken or slaughtered, and family members terrorized. At least two county residents were "murdered in cold blood." One, the prominent planter James C. Bennett, was brutally killed at his home between Lilesville and Morven. Bishop Atkinson reported that "he was shot at the door of his own house because he did not give up his watch and money, which had been previously taken from him by another party." The second victim, a Mr. James Cottingham, was similarly killed when unable to produce valuables that had already been stolen from him.[24]

March 4 (Saturday)

In the nation's capital Pres. Abraham Lincoln and Vice-Pres. Andrew Johnson took their oaths of office. Lincoln's brief inaugural address sounded a reassuring note of conciliation, and the general mood of the city's residents and visitors was noticeably more elevated than had been the case four years earlier.[25] At Cheraw and near Sneedsborough, Union soldiers of the right and left wings respectively celebrated the inaugural ceremonies vicariously and in their own ways—some with pyrotechnic displays, others with wines confiscated from local cellars.[26] Capt. Dexter Horton of Michigan was very much aware of the day's festivities in Washington as he trudged through the rain toward Sneedsborough, but he also bore with him, as he walked, a hearty animosity toward the state he was now leaving. He wrote in his diary: "March 4: A gala day at Washington, the inauguration of President Lincoln. . . . Reached the North Carolina line about 3 o'clock. Goodbye land of secesh. Your country is now nearly desolate. May you relent early."[27]

The entire left wing, in fact, was moving slowly through the rain toward Sneedsborough, the wagon trains of whole divisions becoming so deeply mired as to "baffle all the attempts of the mules to extricate them."[28] Capt. George W. Pepper of Ohio recorded that the day had "been one of the hardest upon the men and animals we have yet experienced."[29]

Gen. John W. Geary of the Twentieth Corps shared Pepper's view of the wretched roads and dismal weather, but he was palpably pleased with the success of his division's foragers as they combed Anson County: "Encamped near Sneedsborough, covering the plank road which runs from Wadesborough to Cheraw. The roads were of the worst description, the entire surface of the country being quicksand, which had to be corduroyed. Country poor and thinly settled, yet our foragers brought in abundant supplies, mostly from the regions between us and Wadesborough. . . ."[30]

Gen. Joseph E. Johnston began the tentative relocation of his headquarters from Charlotte to Fayetteville, "considering the latter as a better point to obtain quick intelligence of the enemy's movements, and to direct those of the Confederate troops." Beauregard remained behind "to protect the line of railroad from Charlotte to Danville, and to send the troops of the Army of Tennessee, as they arrived, to Smithfield, by railroad."[31]

Hardee, meanwhile, was acting under existing orders to move his army northward to Greensboro after crossing the Pee Dee. By day's end he had proceeded as far as Rockingham. While there he received new orders to turn his army toward Fayetteville in advance of Sherman's forces.[32]

A lengthy cavalry engagement between troops from the commands of Judson Kilpatrick and Gen. Joseph Wheeler developed at Phillips Crossroads. The Confederates held the upper hand for most of the day but were then driven back by superior artillery.[33]

Federal raids continued in Anson County and particularly in Wadesboro. "[S]everal parties" visited the town and resumed "the search for valuables left unfinished by the parties who preceeded them."[34] The largest and presumably the most destructive of those "several parties" was a contingent from the Ninth Michigan Cavalry under the command of Maj. J. G. McBride. McBride's terse instructions and his success in carrying them out were reported at the end of the day by his superior, Col. George S. Acker: "Early in the day, in compliance with orders from division headquarters, a scouting party of 100 men, under command of Major McBride, was sent to Wadesborough, nine miles, with written instructions to 'clean out the town.' The major proceeded to Wadesborough, destroyed a grist-mill, sawmill, tannery, large government stables, and all other public property."[35] In addition to those places of business destroyed outright, several were broken into; and private citizens were again robbed of their provisions, money, and remaining valuables. Bishop Atkinson, who had endured considerable loss and abuse during the previous day, now saw his chinaware and books destroyed and thrown into the street.[36]

As the bishop of North Carolina experienced this renewed vandalism, the rector of nearby Calvary Episcopal Church was one of several local clergymen to have their churches broken into and robbed. In the Calvary Church records, the Reverend C. F. Bland left the following notation: "This day a portion of General Kilpatrick's command was sent to sack our village, which they did and robbed the church of the few dollars on hand. General Kilpatrick was an officer of Sherman's Army, and was acting under order of his commander-in-chief. This is one of many churches robbed."[37]

As Gen. Joseph E. Johnston moved from Charlotte toward Fayetteville, he established his headquarters at least briefly at Salisbury. It was, unfortunately, while he was there that a boisterous group of Confederate soldiers "gutted" a local grog-shop (Jack Hall's) and otherwise comported themselves in an unseemly manner: "They not only carried off or destroyed two or three barrels of Jack's liquor, but much other property besides, such as flour, meat, decanters, money and valuable papers; altogether inflicting upon him a very heavy loss. And this was done near the centre of town, and almost in the very presence of those conservators of the law, our town police!"[38]

Meanwhile, the increasingly violent bands of Confederate deserters in Randolph and other counties continued their unchecked depredations. A subsequent issue of the *Daily Conservative* of Raleigh carried the following account of the "desperadoes or outlaws" in Guilford County:

On last Saturday night [March 4] they visited a lone widow woman in the southeastern part of Guilford, supposing she had a large amount of money, threatening her with awful punishment if she did not get it. . . . She still refused to give them her money, they tied a rope around her neck and told her they would hang her till she was dead which frightened her very much. She then went and gave it to the wretches. They visited Spring Dale Academy, burned the house, books and all the apparatus belonging to the Academy.[39]

Indeed, it was on or about this date that a particularly brazen group of Confederate deserters accosted and robbed engineers attached to the command of Gen. William J. Hardee. The *Greensboro Patriot* reported that "A band of deserters [had] captured Gen. Hardee's engineer corps in Randolph County" recently, "stripping them of their clothing, and robbing them of all the money in their possession."[40]

March 5 (Sunday)

The Seventeenth Corps completed its crossing of the Pee Dee at Cheraw, and the Fifteenth began crossing later in the day. The Twentieth Corps marched southward from Sneedsborough, leaving the Fourteenth Corps there to await completion of a pontoon bridge over the swollen stream. Kilpatrick's cavalry, well to the north, also prepared for the crossing.[41]

The continuing movement of Union troops now brought some measure of relief to the citizens of Anson County. The editor of the Wadesboro *Argus* noted that, after three days, the number of unwelcome guests began "to fall off." There was, however, one last, brief raid on Wadesboro, where the raiders encountered advance scouts from Wheeler's cavalry. The Federal raiding party set fire to "the guard house in the rear of the Court House as a parting token," leaving one of their number fatally wounded "just in front of the Masonic Hall."[42]

Some impression of the cumulative despolation and suffering in the rural areas of Anson County is conveyed in the diary of Esther Alden of South Carolina, who several days after the Federals' departure undertook a journey into that county to visit a family plantation:

Anything more frightful than the day's journey I cannot imagine. First of all was the terrible state of the road, which was one continued slough of despondency; then the perpetual sight of dead creatures and the sickening stench arising therefrom; the misery, desolation and hunger of the people living on the road. It is like some horrid nightmare. When I shut my eyes I see nothing but creatures and human beings in agony. . . . The houses which we passed were all shut up—no look of life about them. . . .

The wanton destruction in . . . [our own] house is extraordinary. Everything is cut to pieces with swords; not a chair remains whole; the white marble from the cellarette lies on the floor in fragments, the cellarette itself has been chopped with swords or hatchets, two exquisite figures of Night and Morning lie on the floor in a thousand pieces; two very handsome old mirrors are shattered. It is enough to make mamma ill—things she has been careful of, things many of which have accompanied her from youth to age destroyed.[43]

Soon after assuming command from Beauregard, Gen. Joseph E. Johnston was dismayed to learn that he, much like Sherman, would be expected to provide for his troops "from the land." Although vast quantities of provisions had been collected in North Carolina and were then stored in various depots, they were reserved for Gen. Robert E. Lee's troops in Virginia.[44] Indeed, Lee's own dispatch to Johnston on this date could scarcely have been more concise and to the point: "Endeavor to supply your army by collecting subsistance through the country. That at depots is necessary for the Army of Northern Virginia."[45] Understandably,

Johnston felt at the time and later that the restrictions in regard to supplies stemmed from "excessive caution" and that they deprived his outnumbered forces of the mobility they so desperately needed.[46]

Meanwhile, in Salisbury, not content with the escapades of the previous evening, a group of Confederate soldiers attempted additional "raids" on local business establishments. A chagrined *Carolina Watchman* carried the following notice of the affair:

We learn that a large number of soldiers collected together in our streets Sunday night for the purpose of making "raids" on such buildings in town as were supposed to contain goods and wares suited to their taste. But the Town Police, assisted by a company of infantry sent up from the Garrison, very soon brought an end to all their schemes.—Some slight resistance was made, several persons damaged and some running done, but 35 or 40 of the disturbers of the peace (two or three officers among them) were arrested and sent to the Guard House. We suppose they will be held to a proper accountability.[47]

A far more serious incident—involving Confederate deserters rather than soldiers—occurred during that same evening in Chatham County. Outraged by recent crimes in their area, armed residents of the Mount Vernon Springs community confronted a band of deserters and gained a decided advantage during the ensuing gunfire. The armed residents killed two of the deserters on the spot and caused three others to be jailed in Pittsboro. The *Fayetteville Observer* reported that the deserters "had just robbed the house of a Mrs. Dark, whose husband is in the service and who has no man at her house to protect her."[48]

March 6 (Monday)

The Fifteenth and Twentieth Corps and Sherman himself crossed over the pontoon bridge at Cheraw, joining the Seventeenth, which had crossed during the previous day. Further upstream, at Sneedsborough, the Fourteenth Corps completed its delayed crossing. Still further upstream, Kilpatrick's cavalry moved to the east side of the Pee Dee, then toward nearby Rockingham. With his entire army east of the Pee Dee, Sherman then deployed each element for the march on Fayetteville, traveling himself with the Fifteenth Corps:

On the 6th of March I crossed the Pedee, and all the army marched for Fayetteville: the Seventeenth Corps kept well to the right to make room; the Fifteenth Corps marched by a direct road, the Fourteenth Corps also followed a direct road from Sneedsboro', where it had crossed the Pedee; and the Twentieth Corps, which had come into Cheraw for the convenience of the pontoon-bridge, diverged to the left, so as to enter Fayetteville next after the Fourteenth Corps, which was appointed to lead into Fayetteville. Kilpatrick held his cavalry still farther to the left rear on the roads from Lancaster, by way of Wadesboro' and New Gilead, so as to cover our trains from Hampton's and Wheeler's cavalry, who had first retreated toward the north.[49]

Dressed in Confederate uniforms, Gen. Oliver O. Howard's chief scout and a few selected men left the main columns to reconnoiter eastward as far as Laurel Hill. There they found only a small force of Confederate militiamen on picket duty, as well as a general expectation among the civilian population that Sherman's intended objective was Charlotte. Indeed, that erroneous but persistent impression still prevailed widely, even in Fayetteville itself.[50]

Sherman, of course, had his objective firmly in mind as he and his army proceeded eastward. He expressed the hope, however, that it might be achieved with little military resistance and with minimal destruction of private property. With that hope in mind, he directed the following order to the left wing's overall commander, Gen. Henry W. Slocum:

I propose your command should first enter and occupy Fayetteville and secure the bridge if possible, otherwise to make a lodgement across with pontoons. . . . On approaching Fayetteville you may give it out that if the bridge is destroyed we will deal harshly with the town, but if there be no positive resistance and if the enemy spare the bridge I wish the town to be dealt with generously. Of course we will dispose of all public stores and property but will spare private houses. Use wheat, corn, meal, bacon, animals, wagons, etc., needed by your command, but try and keep the foragers from insulting families by word or rudeness. It might be well to instruct your brigade commanders that we are now out of South Carolina and that a little moderation may be of political consequence to us in North Carolina.[51]

Unfortunately, Sherman's hopes and expectations with regard to Fayetteville were to prove far too sanguine.

It was on this day that Gen. Joseph E. Johnston's command authority over all Confederate troops in North Carolina, including those previously under the command of Gen. Braxton Bragg, went formally into effect. With that enlargement of Johnston's authority, the number of men now directly available to him increased by roughly ten thousand—still too few to oppose Sherman's army in its entirety.[52]

Serious problems with Confederate deserters in the central and western portions of the state continued and proliferated. The *Fayetteville Observer* noted that it had "become a common occurrence for the stage coach on the High Point road, to be attacked, and any deserter that might be on transportation turned loose."[53] The same paper also informed its readers that bands of deserters had committed several recent outrages in Watauga and Caldwell Counties.[54]

March 7 (Tuesday)

With Kilpatrick's cavalry protecting their exposed flanks, large elements of Sherman's left wing trod North Carolina soil for the first time on this day. Meanwhile, the right wing and Sherman himself drew very near to the state line by nightfall along a more southerly route.[55] Writing in his diary that evening, Maj. George Ward Nichols of Sherman's staff recorded the following summary of the day's troop movements: "The army is now all upon the east bank of the Peedee, marching upon roads leading due east. Kilpatrick covers the extreme left. . . . The four grand columns of infantry are all south of Kilpatrick, covering a strip of country forty miles in width. All the corps commanders report abundance of forage and supplies, and the numerous streams which empty into the Peedee have excellent water power, with flour mills situated at points convenient for the army. . . ."[56]

In welcome contrast with the continual rains of the past several weeks, the weather, Nichols reported, was "clear and delightful."[57] Nichols noted that he had "seen dust rising over the moving columns for the first time since we left Savannah."[58] Both the refugees and the soldiers were invigorated to some extent by the change in weather, but the increasing size of the refugee trains was siphoning off progressively higher proportions of the army's supplies and provisions. Indeed, Sherman had already decided that he would have to rid himself of the refugee burden as soon as he reached Fayetteville.[59]

As Kilpatrick's cavalry moved eastward through the sand hills and into the Coastal Plain, it encountered scattered elements of both Wheeler's and Butler's cavalry divisions. Significant skirmishes occurred near Rockingham and at Southwest Creek, closer to Fayetteville. In the town of Rockingham itself, foragers from Sherman's left wing clashed sharply with a party of Butler's cavalrymen.[60]

As Sherman himself approached the North Carolina line, his corps commanders issued new orders to regulate foraging and better protect the lives and property of civilians in and near the army's path. Clearly, both Sherman and his commanding officers felt and believed that North Carolina bore far less responsibility than South Carolina for plunging the nation into civil war; and it was widely hoped that milder and more conciliatory behavior might reap beneficial results in the state that lay before them. Capt. George W. Pepper of Ohio, chronicling in his diary the movements of Sherman's army, clearly shared those sentiments: "Of course, it would be necessary to take of whatever food was needed for army consumption, even from the people of North Carolina; but I think the general feeling of the command was more favorable to the people of North Carolina than to those of the state we had just left."[61]

An order issued at Sneedsborough at the behest of General Slocum, overall commander of the left wing, likewise reflected that leniency: "All officers and soldiers of this command are reminded that the State of North Carolina was one of the last States that passed the ordinance of secession, and that from the commencement of the war there has been in this State a strong Union party. . . . It should not be assumed that the inhabitants are enemies to our Government, and it is to be hoped that every effort will be made to prevent any wanton destruction of property, or any unkind treatment of citizens."[62]

Sherman reiterated this less vindictive outlook in his order to Kilpatrick with regard to Fayetteville. Again, however, he stipulated that no resistance be offered and that the Clarendon Bridge over the Cape Fear be left intact: "If the people will spare the bridge, I want all to be easy on the citizens, but if they burn bridges or bother us we must go the whole figure. . . . Deal as moderately and fairly by the North Carolinians as possible, and fan the flame of discord already subsisting between them and their proud cousins of South Carolina."[63]

Meanwhile, as Sherman's forces moved toward Fayetteville, major troop movements were also occurring to the north and east. Gen. Jacob D. Cox had established an important base of supplies at New Bern, and his troops had made considerable progress in repairing the severed railroad connection between that port and Goldsboro. Related repair efforts also were under way from Goldsboro southward to Wilmington. At Southwest Creek, near Kinston, Cox's forces came in contact with entrenched Confederates under Gen. Braxton Bragg's overall command. It was there that Bragg hoped to check the Federal advance inland from the coast. The fighting of this day, however, was of a preliminary and indecisive nature. The major clash of arms was still to come.[64]

Federal troops carried out several successful and destructive raids on this day as they moved eastward, especially in Richmond and present-day Scotland Counties. At three o'clock in the afternoon a contingent of Union soldiers entered Laurinburg, setting fire to the depot and associated railroad properties. The men then returned southward to the Springfield community, "where they encamped in considerable force."[65]

At Rockingham, troopers from Kilpatrick's cavalry division returned to the scene of the previous day's skirmish. While there they destroyed a cotton factory, a shipment of hides, and a small quantity of firearms.[66] At nearby Marks Station, on the Wilmington, Charlotte, and Rutherfordton Railroad, troops from the Twentieth Corps under Gen. J. W. Geary "destroyed three-quarters of a mile of track, and a quantity of new iron rails which were piled up for shipment to other points." In addition, Geary reported that his men had destroyed "several large resin factories."[67]

Indeed, it is probable that this day witnessed the first of several deliberately set fires in the great pine forests of central and eastern North Carolina—fires that severely damaged the state's venerable naval stores industry and provided spectacle for legions of onlookers. Doubtless, too, these rapidly moving and far-ranging fires also resulted in the incineration of many homes and outbuildings, which otherwise might have survived Sherman's march unscathed. Perhaps the most vivid and ingenuous description of the fires was that provided by Capt. Daniel Oakey of Massachusetts, who found himself both intrigued and saddened by the "wanton destruction":

The effect of these peculiar watch-fires on every side, several feet above the ground, with flames licking their way up the tall trunks, was peculiarly striking and beautiful. But it was sad to see this wanton destruction of property, which, like the firing of the resin pits, was the work of "bummers" who were marauding through the country committing every sort of outrage. There was no restraint except with the column or the regular foraging parties. We had no communications, and could have no safe-guards. The country was necessarily left to take care of itself, and became a "howling waste." The "coffee coolers" of the Army of the Potomac were archangels compared to our "bummers," who often fell to the tender mercies of Wheeler's cavalry, and were never heard of again, earning a fate richly deserved.[68]

While in Rockingham on this day, Kilpatrick received information that the Confederates had arrested three local citizens for burning bridges over the nearby Lumber River and thereby delaying the movement of Hardee's troops eastward. He also received a report, however, that some eight hundred Federal prisoners had sworn allegiance to the Confederacy and that Hardee was now using them for road work in support of the Confederate war effort.[69]

It was on this same day that the editor of the *Western Democrat* saw fit to come to the defense of Kilpatrick's old nemesis, Joseph Wheeler. Throughout much of Georgia and South Carolina, Wheeler and his command had gained a notorious reputation for depredations against defenseless civilians; and it must be acknowledged that this ill fame had at least partially been earned. Indeed, Wheeler's past record of lax discipline had been the principal reason for Gen. Wade Hampton's elevation above him as Sherman approached North Carolina soil. Still, the accusations continued. Keenly aware of all this, the Charlotte editor stated his belief that at least some of the crimes charged against Wheeler's men had been committed by others:

We are disposed to think that "Wheeler's Cavalry" have been, to a great extent, unjustly censured. All thieving that is done, or depredations of any sort that have been committed, is charged upon Wheeler's cavalry, although in some instances, it is known that they were far away. We learn that Wheeler's men have been close on the flanks of the enemy ever since they left Columbia and we know (from official reports) that they have fought the enemy wherever opportunity offered. . . . We suspect that the sins of others are often laid on Wheeler's men.[70]

March 8 (Wednesday)

Traveling with the Fifteenth Corps, Sherman crossed finally into North Carolina and proceeded as far eastward as Laurel Hill. The Seventeenth Corps, meanwhile, marched a short distance further to encamp along the upper reaches of the Lumber River. The left wing and Kilpatrick's cavalry continued in the direction of Fayetteville along a more northerly route. During the evening hours Kilpatrick's troops crossed over the Lumber River and encountered the rear guard of Hardee's forces near Solemn Grove (Monroe's Crossroads) in present-day Hoke County. That location would be the scene of a major cavalry engagement two days later. Further eastward, a few detachments and several officers from Hardee's corps proceeded as far as Fayetteville and began entering the city.[71]

The previous day's respite from rain came to an end, and the roads again became muddy and difficult of passage.[72] Despite the miserable weather and traveling conditions, however, Major Nichols noted a distinct contrast between his North Carolina surroundings and those of the state he had just left behind:

The line which divides South and North Carolina was passed by the army this morning. It was not in our imagination alone that we could see a difference between the two states. The soil is not superior to that near Cheraw, but the farmers are a vastly different class of men. . . .

The real difference between the two regions lies in the fact that the plantation owners work with their own hands, and do not think themselves degraded thereby. For the first time since we bade farewell to salt water I have to-day seen an attempt to manure land. The army has passed through thirteen miles or more of splendidly-managed farms; the corn and cotton fields are nicely plowed and furrowed; the fences are in capital order; the barns are well built; the dwellinghouses are cleanly, and there is that air of thrift which shows that the owner takes a personal interest in the conduct of affairs.[73]

It was Nichols's distinct impression, too, that the behavior and discipline of Sherman's soldiers had improved since crossing into North Carolina, although it is clear that his expectations of strong Unionist sentiment were overly inflated:

The conduct of the soldiers is perceptibly changed. I have seen no evidence of plundering; the men keep their ranks closely; and, more remarkable yet, not a single column of fire or smoke which a few days ago marked the positions of heads of column, can be seen upon the horizon. Our men seem to understand that they are entering a state which has suffered for its Union sentiment, and those inhabitants would gladly embrace the old flag again if they have the opportunity, which we mean to give them, or I am mistaken as to our future campaigns.[74]

Just as General Slocum had issued an order restraining the left wing's foraging activities in North Carolina, so too did General Howard now attempt to govern the conduct of the right wing in gathering food and supplies in the state. As had been the case with Slocum's order, the directive Howard issued was in keeping with Sherman's avowed intentions of pursuing a more moderate, less destructive course in North Carolina. Indeed, the order was issued at Laurel Hill, where Sherman's headquarters were located:

Hereafter but one mounted foraging party, to consist of sixty men with the proper number of commissioned officers, will be allowed for each division. The division commanders will be careful to select reliable officers for the command of these parties, who shall be held strictly accountable for the conduct of their men. Whenever it may be necessary to send a party from the main body, a commissioned officer will be sent in charge, but in no case will it be allowed to go in advance of the infantry advance guard of the leading division, or more than five miles from either flank of the column. . . .

If not already done, there will be organized for each division a provost guard, to consist of as many picked and resolute men as the division commanders may deem sufficient. On the march the guard of the leading division will march with the advance guard, and establish guards at every house on the line of march, which will be relieved by the guard of each succeeding division as it comes up.[75]

It was while at Laurel Hill that Sherman took steps to communicate with Federal troops at Wilmington and to arrange for a conjunction of his own forces with those of Gen. John M. Schofield at Goldsboro. Sherman ordered two messengers to Wilmington by different routes with identical dispatches, even though he had not yet received definite word that Wilmington had fallen.[76]

In fact, Schofield arrived at New Bern from Wilmington on the same day that Sherman dispatched his messengers. Because much of his Twenty-third Corps was still en route to the Kinston area from the south, Schofield ordered Cox to maintain a cautious defensive posture while awaiting its arrival. Meanwhile, Bragg's opposing forces near Kinston had been augmented during the early morning hours by the arrival of some two thousand troops under Gen. D. H. Hill.[77]

Well before noon, Bragg ordered both Hill's troops and those of Gen. Robert F. Hoke to cross Southwest Creek en masse and to strike the Federals' right and left flanks respectively. By day's end the Confederates had significantly advanced their positions and had taken nearly one thousand prisoners.[78]

Federal raids in the present Scotland County area were fewer and less vigorously opposed than during the previous day. Troops in the vicinity of Laurel Hill destroyed the Murdock Morrison gun factory, presumably to prevent its further use as a supplier of Confederate arms.[79] Less necessary from a military standpoint was the ransacking of the meeting place of the Richmond Temperance and Literary Society near Wagram. It was probably the events of this day that secretary J. M. Johnson later recorded in the society's minutes:

> After a considerable interruption caused by the unwelcome visit of Sherman's thieves, the Society meets again. And, of course, when God's own house is outraged by Yankee brutes, temples of morality and science will not be respected.
>
> We find the ornaments of our fair little Hall shattered and ruined; our books shelves empty; the grove strewn with fragments of valuable, precious volumes; the speeches and productions of members who are sleeping in silent graves, torn and trampled in the mire "as pearls before swine."[80]

According to at least one contemporary source, an occurrence far more violent and tragic took place on or about this date in the Laurinburg area. Capt. David P. Conyngham, a war correspondent for the *New York Herald*, alleged in his chronicle of Sherman's march that a number of slaves in the vicinity were summarily executed in order to prevent their escape to freedom:

> The slaves around Laurensburg [Laurinburg], at the opening of our campaign through Carolina, had organized a party with the intention of forcing their way to our lines. The plot was discovered, and at one of their meetings they were surrounded by parties of the home guards, captured, and after a kind of mock trial, twenty-five were hung. Captain Robert Johnson, Colonel Robert Dacker, and Captain Tate, of Richmond County, were the leaders in this barbarous business.[81]

March 9 (Thursday)

Continuing eastward, Sherman and the Fifteenth Corps ended a miserable day's march near a small Presbyterian church at Bethel. There, in Sherman's words, he and others "took refuge in a terrible storm of rain, which poured all night, making the roads awful."[82] General Frank P. Blair, meanwhile, with the Seventeenth Corps, moved slowly during the day to the Raft Swamp vicinity, approximately twenty miles southwest of Fayetteville. The Fourteenth and Twentieth Corps continued eastward from the Lumber River along a more northerly route, reaching a point approximately equidistant from Fayetteville by nightfall.[83] The end of the day found Kilpatrick and his cavalry encamped at Solemn Grove. Discovering their position during the night, Wade Hampton laid careful plans for a surprise attack at sunrise on the following morning.[84]

Near Kinston, the previous day's battle between the forces of Jacob Cox and Braxton Bragg resumed on a smaller scale, with intermittent skirmishes throughout the day. Nevertheless, decisive fighting did not occur until the following morning.[85] In the little Presbyterian church at Bethel, an anonymous Union wag left mock instructions in the pulpit Bible for the Reverend "Mr. McNeil's" next sermon. Otherwise, no harm appears to have befallen the building or its grounds.[86]

Several rural communities and homesteads, however, did not emerge unscathed from Union occupation of the general area. In the Philadelphus community of nearby Robeson County, one resident wrote that Sherman's men "visited us in torrents," comporting themselves like "escaped fiends from the lower regions."[87]

At Antioch, Sherman himself prevented a party of Union soldiers from setting fire to the home of Daniel S. Morrison but did nothing to prevent the theft of Morrison's chickens or the jewelry belonging to his wife.[88] Another resident of the Antioch community was careful to distinguish between the behavior of the bummers and that of the soldiers who followed in their wake. The "scouts," she reported, "destroyed more than the real army."[89] Indeed, this same resident was rather favorably impressed by the efforts of the regular troops at Antioch to protect her home and family members from harm during their brief stay: "The officers were kind enough to furnish a guard upon request. The General's tent was at our front gate, my mother asked him for a guard for the night; he sent two who slept in the house, who seemed to be perfect gentlemen. We were not molested in any way during the night. These men of whom I speak were from Illinois."[90]

At Glen Burnie, the plantation home of the Worth family, Miss Nellie Worth recalled vividly a visitation by the bummers, possibly from Blair's Seventeenth Corps:

> Papa ran to the swamp as soon as he saw them coming, and they were almost frantic with rage when they found he had left them and started in the woods to find him and swore by all the saints in heaven that they would kill him if they found him. . . . The rascals all came in, and in less than ten minutes the house was stripped of almost every thing. . . . One of them came to me to know where . . . [the watches] were, I of course refused to tell, he then immediately presented a pistol to my head and swore he would take my life if I did not tell him. . . .[91]

At Glen Burnie, as at Antioch, however, civilian observers drew a clear distinction between advance troops (or bummers) acting on their own and the men who followed under an officer's close supervision. The residents of Glen Burnie were clearly relieved and grateful when a Union officer at last made his presence felt:

> There was no officer with the first men that came, and our drooping spirits were revived about one o'clock by the sight of a Yankie officer. He came in the house and introduced himself as Lt. Bracht . . . , Mamma and I appealed to him for protection and he soon had order restored in the house, and gave us a guard. I think he was very much of a gentleman. He was very kind to me, that was something I did not expect. . . . He came too late to save any of our property that the Yankies wanted. They carried off every single thing we had to eat, did not leave a grain of corn or coffee, or anything that would sustain life for one day, they found all our silver and took every knife, fork and spoon we had in the world.[92]

Unfortunately, the Federal soldiers in the area could not resist the impulse to torch the surrounding forests. This same Glen Burnie resident reported that as the troops left, "they set the Pine Woods on fire all around us."[93]

At Lumberton, the Robeson County seat, mounted infantrymen from Blair's Seventeenth Corps destroyed several designated facilities and then broadened the scope of their activities to include the pillaging of private residences. Among the facilities destroyed were the local railroad depot, several boxcars, approximately one mile of track, and bridges over the Lumber River.[94] The Reverend Washington S. Chaffin noted in his diary that Federal horsemen stole his wife's watch and his horse, fired on his neighbor in the street, and in general "entered many houses and committed many depredations."[95]

Meanwhile, an increasingly desperate John M. Worth was writing to his brother, Jonathan, beseeching him to intercede with Governor Vance and see that something be done to relieve the conditions of near anarchy in Randolph County:

> I want to urge with all my power I can that Gov. Vance send a man as promised to take care of what I have been calling the better class of deserters. If he does not do it we are all gone. . . . The County is full of all sorts of folks moving from Sherman and we are being swallowed up. If the Gov. will send at once a man authorized to enlist the deserters I shall have a little hope except I am bothered with all sorts of trouble sick, wounded and hungry, robbers and Rangers and every other sort of trouble.[96]

March 10 (Friday)

The four corps of Sherman's army trudged slowly through deep mud and heavy rain to points roughly ten miles west of Fayetteville. Despite the miserable conditions, Sherman and the Fifteenth Corps managed to cover a respectable thirteen miles; the Fourteenth Corps, on the other hand, progressed only three miles during the entire day.[97]

Kilpatrick, meanwhile, remained at Solemn Grove with his brigades deployed in such a way as to intercept Hampton's cavalry troops as they moved eastward toward Fayetteville and a juncture with Hardee's infantry corps. Confederate reconnaissance of the previous evening, however, had revealed Kilpatrick's whereabouts and thereby thwarted his carefully laid plan. Just before sunrise Hampton's cavalry forces attacked Kilpatrick's sleeping camp, catching the Federal cavalrymen completely by surprise and driving them into the woods. Kilpatrick himself rushed from the home of Charles Monroe only partially clothed. Soon, however, the Federal troops rallied, returned to the scene of the attack, and drove the Confederates off. Though Hampton's forces were defeated at the close of the encounter, he had succeeded in delaying Kilpatrick's progress eastward and had therefore given Hardee and his men sufficient time to reach Fayetteville safely and in reasonably good order. Indeed, it was Hampton's cavalry, rather than Kilpatrick's, that succeeded in reaching Fayetteville that night.[98]

Although Gen. Oliver O. Howard had issued an order two days earlier regarding the foraging activities of all components of the right wing, Gen. F. P. Blair now imposed similar restrictions on the Seventeenth Corps specifically. As others had done before him, Blair drew a clear distinction between North Carolinians and their neighbors to the south:

> The State of North Carolina is to a great extent loyal, and as such, a marked difference should be made in the manner in which we treat the people and the manner in which those in South Carolina were treated. Nothing should be taken from them except what is absolutely necessary for the use of the army, and to this end the following regulations will be strictly enforced: A foraging party for each division will be organized, to consist of sixty

men and the proper number of commissioned officers. Reliable officers will be selected for these parties, officers who can and will control their men, and they will be held strictly responsible for the acts of the men. The men will not be permitted to enter dwelling houses under any circumstances. They must be kept together and at all times under the eye of a commissioned officer. If it is necessary to detach a portion of the party they will be sent under charge of a commissioned officer. These men will take nothing but what is necessary— that is, animals, food for the command, and forage for the stock. . . . Provost-marshals of divisions will patrol their line of march with a detachment of mounted men, and they will arrest and dismount all mounted men found away from the line of march, unless they are regularly detailed foragers with their officers complying with this order. . . . All officers are charged with the execution of this order and will arrest any men found violating it.[99]

At Kinston the confrontation between Cox's Federals and Bragg's Confederates ground to a halt. After several unsuccessful assaults on Union positions along a broad front, Bragg's forces withdrew toward Goldsboro and an anticipated juncture beyond with the troops of Gen. Joseph E. Johnston. The three-day affair near Kinston had by no means halted the Federal movement inland to link up with Sherman's advancing army; it had only delayed it temporarily.[100]

The main body of General Hardee's corps reached Fayetteville during the afternoon and evening hours, followed closely by Hampton's battle-weary cavalrymen.[101] Though the town's residents provided a warm reception to the arriving Confederates, they could not help but notice the large numbers of sick and wounded among the ranks. Nor could they fail to notice the looks of concern etched in the faces both of officers and enlisted men. One local resident recorded the following memories and observations:

> The night of the 10th was clear, with the moon shining brightly. The columns of infantry continued to march by, looking so worn and ragged, poor fellows, as from time to time a few of them would come in for rest and refreshment. A party of general officers came in and examined a map, looking anxious and low spirited. A party of young men . . . had been with us all day, some of their number being sick. After all was quiet they tied their horses under our windows and we kept guard over them while their masters slept on the floor. How sorry we all felt for the poor boys, and how often wondered if they all lived to get home or perished in the single battle that was fought before the surrender.[102]

At least one detachment of Union troops diverged from the normal line of march to destroy a textile mill in the nearby Rockfish community. In carrying out their orders, these mounted infantrymen from Blair's Seventeenth Corps "destroyed the machinery and burned the factory buildings." The unit's commanding officer reported, moreover, that the facility "was one of the largest in the State, having 318 looms."[103]

Meanwhile, conditions in the central Piedmont continued to deteriorate, with residents of rural areas especially being victimized by marauding bands of deserters. From Ingle's Mills in Guilford County, a correspondent brought the increasingly serious situation to the attention of a Raleigh newspaper editor:

> Dear Sir:—I write you a few lines to apprise you of the many depredations that are committed upon the citizens of Guilford and Randolph. The desperadoes or outlaws are robbing the citizens of Randolph and Guilford; they are supposed to be deserters. . . . They went to

an aged citizen's house in Randolph, a Mr. Lutterlough, pillaged his house, burned all his valuable papers, set his house on fire several times, but he begged the Captain of the thieves to put it out, and they put it out.[104]

March 11 (Saturday)

Sherman's army now converged on Fayetteville from the south and west during the morning hours. Scouts entering the city in advance of the main columns were attacked by a small contingent of Confederate cavalry and suffered several casualties as they retreated. The remaining Confederate cavalrymen then crossed over the Cape Fear River to follow Hardee's troops northward, burning the bridge behind them that Sherman "had hoped to save."[105]

Whole divisions from the Fourteenth and Seventeenth Corps then entered Fayetteville with little resistance aside from sharpshooter fire. Once there, each corps in turn received the surrender of the city from Mayor Archibald McLean. According to prior arrangement, however, most of the troops then withdrew, leaving as an occupying force only Gen. Absalom Baird's Third Division of the Fourteenth Corps. The vast majority of Sherman's army encamped just outside Fayetteville. Sherman himself established temporary headquarters at the former United States Arsenal, which had been seized from the Federal government some four years earlier.[106]

Once in possession of the city, Sherman acted at once to construct pontoon bridges across the Cape Fear so that his army could continue its march toward Goldsboro. He ordered that one bridge be built near the structure destroyed by the retreating Confederates and another approximately four miles downstream.[107] Sherman also issued specific directives regarding the destruction of key facilities in and near Fayetteville. Kilpatrick's cavalry was to destroy "railroad trestles, depots, mills, and factories as far up as lower Little River." Col. O. M. Poe was "charged with the utter demolition of the arsenal building and everything pertaining to it," while chief ordnance officer T. G. Baylor was made responsible for "the destruction of all powder, and ordnance stores, including guns and small arms."[108] Finally, Sherman took initial steps during this first day in Fayetteville to rid his army of the increasingly large and burdensome train of refugees, both black and white. He ordered officers to prepare the refugees to "proceed to Wilmington," accompanied by guard details of one hundred men from each of the two wings.[109]

Hardee's Confederates, meanwhile, had marched northward toward Raleigh after withdrawing from Fayetteville, with Hampton's cavalry functioning as their rear guard. The Confederates' escape from Fayetteville had, in fact, been an extremely narrow one, for Federal troops had been within two hundred yards of the Clarendon Bridge when it was set ablaze. Johnston's orders to Hardee were to move along the Raleigh road, which, for approximately thirty miles, was also the road to Smithfield. The troops under Braxton Bragg and those of the Army of Tennessee were also en route to Smithfield, so that they might intercept a move by Sherman on either Goldsboro or Raleigh.[110]

At Fayetteville, as had been the case with most towns and cities along the route of Sherman's march, the bummers had arrived well in advance of the main columns. Indeed, some of those men had been absent from their units since leaving Cheraw, impatient for the spoils that lay ahead. For a while at least, the activities of bummers inside the city were virtually unrestrained; and numerous business establishments and private residences suffered greatly at their hands. Several citizens were robbed at gunpoint during that early looting. Among them was the Reverend William Hooper, elderly grandson of the William Hooper who had signed the Declaration of Independence for North Carolina.[111]

Miss Alice Campbell of Fayetteville recalled vividly the brief but traumatic interlude between the Confederates' hurried departure and the arrival of Federal regulars:

The enemy seemed to be pouring in by every road that led to our doomed little town. . . . Every yard and every house was teaming with the bummers, who went into our homes— no place was sacred; they even went into our trunks and bureau drawers, stealing everything they could find; our entire premises were ransacked and plundered, so there was nothing left for us to eat, but perhaps a little meal and peas. . . . They went into homes that were beautiful, rolled elegant pianos into the yard with valuable furniture, china, cut glass, and everything that was dear to the heart, even old family portraits, and chopped them up with axes. . . .[112]

So thoroughly had houses in the city been "ransacked and plundered" during that comparatively brief period that it was said to have been doubtful "if all Fayetteville, the next day, could have contributed two whole shirts or a bushel of meal to the relief of the Confederate army."[113]

The bummers in Fayetteville appear to have done their work both thoroughly and with dispatch, perpetrating numerous outrages and creating a scene of general chaos during the brief period available to them. Their activities quickly ended, however, with the arrival of Gen. Absalom Baird's division, which Sherman himself had chosen to occupy the city. Baird, a strict disciplinarian, later acknowledged that conditions upon his arrival had been well out of control:

Having been directed to take command of the city and garrison it with my command the three brigades were at once posted in advantageous positions in the suburbs, and furnished guards not only for public buildings, but for nearly every private house. On our arrival I found the stragglers from all portions of the army who had pushed in with the advanced guards committing many disorders, but as soon as they could be cleared out good order was established and maintained during our stay in the place.[114]

Capt. George W. Pepper of Ohio observed that guards had been "posted at every house in town" and that "everything [was] going on as quietly as ever under the rebel rule."[115] Yet to come in Fayetteville was additional destruction of public and commercial properties, industrial installations, and transportation facilities, but, in the main, private residences and their occupants would be spared further harm.

That conditions in Fayetteville improved significantly with the arrival of Sherman's regular forces and the posting of guards is borne out by the testimony of citizens who experienced the Federal occupation. One terrorized citizen recalled that when bummers burst into her family's residence, it had "seemed as if the lower regions were opened up and the fiends turned loose upon us."[116] The situtation swiftly improved, however, when her aunt enlisted the aid of a young Union officer:

> She then ran out in the street and had the good luck to meet Lieut. McVeagh of Illinois, whom I verily believe was walking ahead of his regiment in order to afford protection to some poor woman who might stand in need of it. He drove the bummers out of the house. . . .
>
> The main body of Sherman's army now began to pass by in martial array with flags flying, the field officers on horseback prancing at the head of the column, the soldiers proudly keeping step to the music of the band. . . . Lieut. McVeagh did all he could to comfort us, even averring that which he did not believe—that the Southern cause was not lost yet. . . .
>
> The guards did their duty well enough, keeping intruders from the house and never failing to call us when any celebrity passed by. . . .[117]

Another Fayetteville resident recalled the courtesy and consideration shown by several of Gen. Oliver O. Howard's officers during their stay in her family's home.[118]

In the countryside surrounding Fayetteville, however, the safeguards available to private dwellings and their occupants were far from adequate. Looting and vandalism spread outward from the city quickly and in all directions. One Fayetteville resident recalled that "As soon as night came on we could see fires in every direction, as all the buildings in the country were burnt."[119] Of course, not "all" or nearly all buildings in the surrounding countryside were burned; but it appears that a fair number of dwelling houses and outbuildings were not only ransacked but put to the torch as well. In general, rural areas near Fayetteville experienced far greater destruction of private property than that which occurred inside the city itself. Moreover, the destruction and associated criminal activities would persist intermittently over the next three days.[120]

The Confederate troops themselves had found it expedient to destroy at least some private property as they made their hasty departure from Fayetteville. They partially destroyed six of the eight steamboats along the river, as well as sizable quantities of cotton stored along the waterfront.[121]

Less justifiable from a military standpoint were two other actions by withdrawing Confederate forces. A retreating cavalryman was said to have shot and wounded a Federal prisoner for no other reason than that he wanted "to kill another d[amne]d Yankee." Reportedly, too, no disciplinary action was taken against the assailant.[122] During this same day, to the west of Fayetteville, a train of severely ill soldiers and possibly refugees was attacked as it followed along behind the Fifteenth Corps. Although there is no indication that any of the sick were killed or wounded, Gen. John E. Smith duly reported the incident:

> The small-pox train which had closed up to within about 500 yards of the command while it was moving out was attacked by a squad of rebel cavalry numbering ten or twelve. The rebels were dressed in Federal uniform, and were supposed to be a portion of our cavalry until they reached the ambulances. They succeeded in getting away two horses. I sent my escort company in pursuit, but they having scattered in the swamp, it was impossible to over take them.[123]

March 12 (Sunday)

Most of Sherman's army was encamped on the outskirts of Fayetteville, while the city itself continued under the occupation of Baird's division of the Fourteenth Corps. For the most part, the citizenry observed the Sabbath in as normal a way as possible. The arsenal still stood, as apparently did most of the public and industrial buildings slated for destruction.

Relative quiet and inactivity seem to have prevailed until just after noon, when the sound of a steamboat whistle made it quickly apparent that the messengers sent from Laurel Hill four days before had gotten through to Wilmington. After months of relative isolation, Sherman and his army were once again in touch with the "outside world." Sherman himself described the context and considerable significance of that event:

Sunday, March 12th, was a day of Sabbath stillness in Fayetteville. The people generally attended their churches, for they were a very pious people . . . and our men too were resting from the toils and labors of six weeks of as hard marching as ever fell to the lot of soldiers. Shortly after noon was heard in the distance the shrill whistle of a steamboat, which came nearer and nearer, and soon a shout, long and continuous, was raised down by the river, which spread farther and farther, and we all felt that it meant a messenger from home. The effect was electric, and no one can realize the feelings unless, like us, he has been for months cut off from all communication with friends, and compelled to listen to the croakings and prognostications of open enemies. . . . Our couriers had got through safe from Laurel Hill, and this was the prompt reply.[124]

Obviously, too, Sherman realized that he was now "in full communication" with Gen. Alfred H. Terry and thus able to choreograph the movement of Union forces on Goldsboro and a likely confrontation with his "special antagonist," Gen. Joseph E. Johnston. In short, he could now prepare fully "for the next and last stage of the war."[125]

Sherman acted quickly to take advantage of his newly opened avenue of communication. At six o'clock in the evening the steamboat began a return trip to Wilmington, carrying with it dispatches from Sherman to Secretary of War Stanton, Generals Terry and Grant, and several others. Sherman's letter to Grant perhaps summarized best the accomplishments of the march thus far, his plans with regard to refugees and the arsenal, and his unwavering determination to reach Goldsboro:

Dear General: We reached this place yesterday at noon. Hardee as usual, retreating across the Cape Fear, burning his bridges; but our pontoons will be up to-day, and, with as little delay as possible, I will be after him to Goldsboro. . . .

The army is in splendid health, condition, and spirits, though we have had foul weather, and roads that would have stopped travel to almost any other body of men I ever heard of. . . . We cannot afford to leave detachments, and I shall therefore destroy this valuable arsenal, so the enemy shall not have its use; and the United States should never again confide such valuable property to a people who have betrayed a trust.

I could leave here to-morrow but I want to clear my columns of the vast crowd of refugees and negroes that encumber us. Some I will send down the river in boats, and the rest to Wilmington by land, under small escort, as soon as we are across Cape Fear River. . . .

Jos. Johnston may try to interpose between me here and Schofield about Newbern; but I think he will not try that, but concentrate his scattered armies at Raleigh, and I will go straight at him as soon as I get our men reclothed and our weapons reloaded. . . .

I expect to make a juncture with General Schofield in ten days.[126]

Apparently there was a considerable amount of pillaging and destruction in the general vicinity of Fayetteville, although conditions inside the city were relatively tranquil. Cumberland County planter James Evans noted briefly in his diary that the weather was "clear and cool" and that there were "Yanks in my house about 11 o'clock A.M." Unfortunately for Evans, the next three days were to prove far worse.[127]

On this day, Federal troops visited other Cumberland County planters and relieved them of their horses, mules, and household valuables. One rural physician "abandoned his house, furniture, negroes, and everything," following a visit by Union soldiers. His terrified wife was reported to have been rendered "nearly a maniac" as a result of the experience.[128]

Meanwhile, in the Piedmont section of the state, conditions of uncertainty and lawlessness continued to prevail in certain locales. In Pittsboro, for example, apprehensive citizens were attempting to conceal food supplies from both the approaching enemy and roving bands of Confederate deserters. In writing to state treasurer Jonathan Worth, a local correspondent briefly summarized their predicament: "People in the community are trying to hide their provisions, expecting the enemy or deserters. It is hard to tell where the safest place is."[129] Unfortunately, making that determination became more difficult during the weeks to come.

March 13 (Monday)

After protracted delays and controversy, an increasingly desperate Confederate Congress approved the enlistment of black soldiers and sent the enabling legislation to Pres. Jefferson Davis for his signature. At this late stage in the war, however, the measure was to have little practical impact.[130]

Meanwhile, Sherman's army remained in and around Fayetteville for much of the day, destroying predetermined targets of military significance, marching in review through the streets, and preparing to cross over to the east side of the Cape Fear River. By late afternoon and evening, some of the Federal troops had made the crossing. Others remained behind, with Baird's division of the Fourteenth Corps still assigned to garrison duty.[131]

Sherman's long-standing desire to rid his army of the swelling refugee trains now took the form of a special field order to prepare for their immediate evacuation:

Maj. John S. Windsor, One hundred and sixteenth Illinois Infantry is hereby detailed to conduct to Wilmington all the refugees, white and black, that now encumber the army. The commanding generals of each wing and of the cavalry will turn over to him all such refugees, with such wagons, horses, and mules, etc. whether captured or public, as may be necessary to facilitate their journey, with a small supply of flour, bacon, and beef cattle. Major Windsor will conduct them to Wilmington and turn them over to the quartermaster's department or Treasury agent, who will dispose of them according to laws or existing orders. A guard of 100 men will be sent from each wing, composed of men entitled to discharge or furlough, provided with their papers, to take effect on arrival at Wilmington.[132]

It was likely not until this time that Sherman fully realized the magnitude of the refugee throng. Once assembled together, the refugees' sheer numbers and destitute condition were sources of wonder and dismay even to Sherman's closest aides:

> While the refugees were scattered throughout the command, it was not easy to ascertain their number. We can now arrive at an approximation. Upon our arrival at Fayetteville, there could not have been less than twenty-five thousand noncombatants who had joined our columns since our departure from Savannah. A very large proportion are negroes, chiefly women and children. As I look back upon the extraordinary march we have made, and reflect upon the stupendous difficulties which have been in the way of successful transit of even so large an army as this, the fact of its accomplishment with twenty-five thousand useless, helpless human beings, devouring food, and clogging every step onward, will remain one of the marvels of military operations.[133]

The huge refugee trains following Sherman's army had contributed greatly to the need for frequent and far-ranging foraging expeditions along the path of march from Savannah northward to Fayetteville and the Cape Fear. Moreover, many of the refugees themselves seized opportunities along the way to forage on their own behalf, not only for food but also for other items left behind by the soldiers who usually preceded them. Many of the animals, furnishings, and miscellaneous conveyances in the refugee trains had been liberated from the refugees' previous homes or from farms and plantations along the line of march. Indeed, still other items of private property would be appropriated as the refugees made their way from Fayetteville to Wilmington.[134]

As Sherman's army prepared to cross the Cape Fear at Fayetteville, Hardee's Confederate forces strengthened their defensive position along the Raleigh road south of Averasboro. Wheeler's cavalry division was deployed nearer Fayetteville along that same road, while Butler's division established a similar position along the Goldsboro road to the east. It was Johnston's plan to be able to intercept Sherman, regardless of which route from Fayetteville the Union commander chose. As advance troops from Kilpatrick's cavalry moved up the Raleigh road, they "skirmished heavily" with elements of Wheeler's force.[135]

It was during this day that the Fayetteville Arsenal and Armory was thoroughly laid in ruins. Having taken a personal interest in the destruction of that facility, Sherman was gratified to report that "Every building was knocked down . . ., and every piece of machinery utterly broken up and ruined."[136] Commenting more generally on the work at Fayetteville, he also reported that "Much valuable property of great use to an enemy was here destroyed or cast into the river."[137] With the Federal occupation of Fayetteville now in its third day, food shortages were growing severe among the townspeople. Capt. Dexter Horton of the Fourteenth Corps noted tersely in his diary that "Everyone" was "out of grub."[138] Indeed, many local larders had been depleted to feed Hardee's Confederates before Sherman's troops arrived on the scene.[139]

Beyond the corporate limits of Fayetteville, the ransacking of private dwellings and various other crimes against the civilian population continued. Planter James Evans, who had been visited by "Yanks" the previous day, now noted the presence of large numbers of both Federal troops and former slaves: "March 13, 1865—clear, over 1000 Yanks in my house during the day and niggers in vast numbers, in the yard and out-houses, stole all of my provisions, and a large amount of other things, all my cattle, horses, mules, Buggy, Wagons, Hogs. . . ."[140]

It was on or about this same day that soldiers identified as Kilpatrick's cavalrymen looted the home of Duncan Murchinson approximately twelve miles from town, barging into the bedroom of a sick child, who succumbed while they were still in the house. The elderly Murchinson had his life threatened and was then dragged half-dressed into a nearby swamp. Inside the house, the cavalrymen destroyed family portraits, demolished furniture, shattered dishes, and emptied molasses into the piano.[141]

At another country residence, some four miles from town, Union troops "tore up, smashed and stole everything they could lay their hands on." They then concluded by "pouring peanut oil over the debris" of the clothing, books, and furnishings that lay strewn about. One soldier, in parting, flung open the family Bible across a mule's back and used it for a saddle as he rode away.[142]

The plantation home of Charles B. Mallett was one of several residences in the Fayetteville area at which the pillaging and destruction by Union soldiers included arson. Mallett himself later recalled their visitation:

The china and glass-ware were all carried out of the house by Federal soldiers, and deliberately smashed in the yard. The furniture—piano, beds, tables, bureaus—were all cut to pieces with axes; the pantries and smoke-houses were stripped of their contents; the negro houses were all plundered; the poultry, cows, horses, etc., were shot down and carried off; and then, after all this, the houses were all fired and burned to the ground.[143]

A similar series of depredations occurred nearby at the plantation of John M. Rose, with the destruction of his dwelling house being only narrowly averted:

The Federal soldiers searched my house from garret to cellar, and plundered it of every thing portable; took all my provisions, emptied the pantries of all stores, and did not leave me a mouthful of any kind of supplies for one meal's victuals. They took all my clothing, even the hat off my head, and the shoes and pants from my person; took most of my wife's and children's clothing, all of our bedding; destroyed my furniture, and robbed all my negroes. At leaving they set fire to my fences, out-houses, and dwelling, which fortunately, I was able to extinguish.[144]

As was the case with Charles B. Mallett, several county residents clearly were not able to "extinguish" the fires that threatened their homes. Rose himself reported that "Nine dwellings were burned to the ground in [his] neighborhood" alone.[145]

In some instances the depredations of Union soldiers outside Fayetteville included assault, torture, and, in one case, murder. Evidence of the murder is once again provided by John M. Rose, who seems to have been referring to his area of the county in particular: "Four gentlemen . . . were hung up by the neck till nearly dead, to force them to tell where valuables were hidden. One was shot in his own house, and died soon after."[146]

With Sherman's troops in and around Fayetteville in such large numbers, their possible movement into surrounding areas became the subject of widespread anxiety and speculation. Raleigh's *Daily Conservative*, therefore, seized the opportunity to assure its Harnett County readers that the rumors of Federal soldiers there had no firm basis in fact: "We have had abundant rumors of the presence of the Yankees in Harnett County, their depredations, burnings, etc. We have conversed with a gentleman, whom we deem reliable, who informs us that no Yankees, so far as he knew, were in Harnett up to the time he left [the night of March 13] . . . , except some stragglers, of which there were present in the county a few from both armies."[147] Ironically, there had been a sharp cavalry skirmish near the Harnett County line the same day that the *Daily Conservative*'s informant had left for Raleigh. Moreover, on the very day that the story appeared, preliminaries for the Battle of Averasboro began.

March 14 (Tuesday)

Many of Sherman's troops continued their assigned duties in Fayetteville, receiving and distributing supplies, destroying designated properties, caring for the sick and wounded, assembling the refugee train, and, finally, crossing over the Cape Fear to join those already assembled on the east bank. Baird's division of the Fourteenth Corps remained behind on garrison duty and was the last to exit the city.[148]

As on the previous day, advance cavalry contingents from Sherman's army came in contact with Confederate rearguard units. At Silver Run Creek on the Raleigh road, entrenched horsemen from Wheeler's division repulsed a Federal reconnaissance unit that "felt its position." Similar fighting occurred on the Goldsboro road between Federal horsemen and elements of Butler's cavalry division.[149]

About midday the steamer *Davidson* arrived from Wilmington, accompanied by two gunboats. Aboard the steamer was Quartermaster General George S. Dodge, who was able to deliver to Sherman sizable quantities of sugar, coffee, and oats but not the clothing he had so hoped for.[150] Once unburdened of their upriver cargos, the *Davidson* and its gunboat escorts were then filled with sick and wounded soldiers bound for Wilmington and more intensive medical care.[151]

Meanwhile, the enormously difficult and complex task of assembling the refugee train continued. The vast majority of the refugees was to proceed to Wilmington by land; but every effort was made, as well, to provide transportation by boat for as many as possible.[152] Indeed, an uncorroborated newspaper account reported that "about 400 negroes and whites were drowned in Cape Fear River, in endeavoring to escape with the Yankees, either from the sinking of a flat or the Yankee officers' cutting the pontoons loose."[153]

Well to the northeast of Fayetteville, Gen. Jacob D. Cox's troops from Schofield's Twenty-third Corps reached as far as Kinston, taking possession of the town with little resistance from Bragg's retreating Confederates. Before leaving, however, Bragg's troops destroyed the ill-fated ram *Neuse* to preclude its falling into enemy hands.[154]

Bragg's retreating troops were now proceeding westward toward Smithfield and a convergence with Gen. Joseph E. Johnston and his still-scattered commands. Elements of the Army of Tennessee were moving simultaneously toward Smithfield from the west, while Hardee's forces had marched northward from Fayetteville toward Averasboro. Even now, Johnston was uncertain as to Sherman's next move.[155]

As the majority of Sherman's army moved out of Fayetteville and across the Cape Fear, their dispersal through the surrounding countryside may actually have increased. Planter James Evans noted the presence of "Thousands of Yanks in the yard and house all day."[156] Another resident of the Fayetteville area characterized the cumulative looting and destruction by Union soldiers during several visits to her family's home:

> There was no place, no chamber, trunk, drawer, desk, garret, closet or cellar that was private to their unholy eyes. Their rude hands spared nothing but our lives. . . . Squad after squad unceasingly came and went and tromped through the halls and rooms of our house day and night during the entire stay of the army.
> At our house they killed every chicken, goose, turkey, cow, calf and every living thing, even to our pet dog. They carried off our wagons, carriage and horses . . . and burned the fences. Our smoke-house and pantry, that a few days ago were well stored . . . , now contain nothing whatever, except a few pounds of meal and flour and five pounds of bacon. They took from old men, women and children alike. . . . Blankets, sheets, quilts, etc., such as it did not suit them to take away they tore to pieces before our eyes.[157]

One of the principal reasons for leaving Baird's division behind in Fayetteville was so that it could oversee the final destruction of the former United States arsenal there. Already that facility lay in ruins, but Sherman now ordered that its scattered remnants be burned.[158] In his diary, Capt. Dexter Horton duly noted the burning of the arsenal ruins, adding that during the course of that work "One private house accidently caught fire." In all probability, the home to which Horton referred was that of William B. Wright.[159]

In fact, the extent of damage to private dwellings in Fayetteville is difficult to determine with precision. One resident recalled that when "The beautiful arsenal was destroyed . . . , several private residences also caught fire and burned down, no help being given to save them."[160] Preponderant evidence, however, suggests that during the burning of the arsenal, Baird's men exercised at least some care to protect nearby residences from harm. Schoolgirl Josephine Worth, for example, recalled vividly and in detail the efforts made to save her family's home on the day the arsenal was burned:

> We got our peck of meal and as we turned homeward we perceived that the Arsenal was in flames. It had been fired at once and presented a frightful appearance, especially to one whose home lay in its immediate vicinity. Frightened out of our wits we hastened home and began moving out, but some officers from Col. Estes' regiment, seeing us from their camp, came and persuaded us it was no use, as they would place a guard in the yard to watch the sparks which were showering in every direction. Gratitude is never out of place, so I take pleasure in mentioning the names of two who were so kind to us on this and other occasions, Capt. J. B. Newton, of Ohio, and W. B. Jacobs, Indiana, although we never made any secret of our opinions. . . .

After all danger of the fire was over and things had quieted down to their normal state, a boy came running to tell us that he saw two men setting our stable on fire. Capt. Carter, from Ohio, had just come in and asked for water to wash. He had been on the roof of a neighbor's house that had caught fire and was so black he could scarcely be told from a "man and brother." He seized the bucket of water that we brought to him and ran to the stable. Sure enough a blue column of smoke was circling up from it. Fortunately he arrived in time to extinguish it or it might have spread to several dwellings.[161]

It was apparently on this same day that the offices of local newspapers were burned to the ground, most notably E. J. Hale's influential *Fayetteville Observer*. In writing of his father's loss, only three months afterward, the editor's son and namesake alleged that Sherman and several of his generals either ordered or witnessed the destruction of both the newspaper office and an adjacent building:

> My father's property, before the war, was easily convertible into $85 to $100,000 in specie. He has not now a particle of property which will bring him a dollar in income. His office, with everything in it, was burned by Sherman's order. Slocum, who executed the order, with a number of other Generals, sat on the verandah of a hotel opposite watching the progress of the flames, while they hobnobbed over wines stolen from our cellar. A fine brick building, adjacent, also belonging to my father, was burned at the same time.[162]

The offices of the *North Carolina Presbyterian* and the *Daily Telegraph*—both less well known than Hale's paper—were destroyed at approximately the same time. Indeed, General Baird stated that he had been responsible for destroying the three newspaper offices and several other facilities in Fayetteville during the last phases of Federal occupation: "Before leaving the town I destroyed 2 iron founderies of some importance, 4 cotton factories, and the printing establishments of 3 rebel newspapers."[163]

It is probable that a good many buildings and business firms in Fayetteville were destroyed during this final day. In addition to those Baird specifically mentioned, it is known that the State Bank building and possibly as many as eleven large warehouses were burned.[164] In accordance with Sherman's earlier orders, all railroad buildings, tanneries, and all gristmills but one were destroyed—the last being left to provide for the local citizenry after the army's departure.[165]

Food, in fact, was becoming very scarce in Fayetteville by the end of Federal occupation. One resident reported that "Many, very many families have not a mouthful to eat."[166] Capt. Dexter Horton, who on the previous day had noted a shortage of "grub," now found the situation still more serious: "March 14: Have been busy all day issuing meal, peanuts, and attending to business generally. . . . Saw many, many sad sights. Weeping mothers with babes in their arms, begging for meal and all such scenes."[167]

Finally, the Federal occupation of Fayetteville drew to a close, and the townspeople would soon be left to resume their ordinary lives as best they could. For some, at least, feelings of bitterness and resentment were tempered by those of acquaintanceship and mutual regard. Young Sally Hawthorne, whose father had lodged Federal officers in their home, left the following account of their departure:

> In the afternoon of that last day of the enemy's sojourn, the officer in command asked my father to get all the household together on one of the front piazzas. All came, but my

mother, who refused. . . . The fine-looking young officer turned to my father, addressing him as Colonel, said he wanted to thank him for the unvarying courtesy they and their men had received. . . . He said that he and his men were leaving with only pleasant memories and he also wanted to assure my father that he would be protected while the army was moving, but that he must do exactly what he was told, or no one would be held responsible. Guards were to be posted all around the property until sunset, at which time all but one man would be relieved, and he would stay on into the night; then he would be called in, at exactly what hour the officer would not say, but the sentry would notify father when he left and father was to have directions given him by that last sentry which he must observe. Finally with his cap in hand, he came up to each one of us and offered his hand, followed by his three aides; then running down the steps, they sprang on their horses and were gone, the men forming in squads following. As they marched past the piazza all looked toward us, some grinning, all very friendly in their different ways. . . .

Far into the night the heavy rumble of moving artillery and the trotting of horses could be heard, and I suppose few people went to bed for fear something might happen— what they knew not. About midnight the sentry knocked on the front door, and on father's opening it, told him now he was going and that orders were that no one was to put his head out till daylight, for, though every precaution had been taken for the safety of the people, there would be many stragglers around, and there would be no sentinels to protect the people. Those were the orders from headquarters. Then he said goodbye, and the last of Sherman's army was gone. . . .[168]

NOTES

1. For additional information on the command structure and characteristics of Sherman's army, see William Tecumseh Sherman, *Memoirs of General W. T. Sherman* (New York: Library of America, 1990 [reprint of 1886 edition]), 749–751; *The War of the Rebellion: A Compilation of the Official Records of the Union and Confederate Armies,* ser. 1, 47, pt. 1:42–55 (hereafter cited as *Official Records . . . Armies*); Joseph T. Glatthaar, *The March to the Sea and Beyond: Sherman's Troops in the Savannah and Carolinas Campaigns* (New York: New York University Press, 1985), 15–38.

2. *Raleigh North Carolina Standard,* March 1, 1865.

3. Sherman, *Memoirs,* 772; *Official Records . . . Armies,* ser. 1, 47, pt. 1:689.

4. Joseph E. Johnston, *Narrative of Military Operations Directed, During the Late War Between the States* (Bloomington: Indiana University Press, 1959; Millwood, N.Y.: Kraus Reprints, 1990), 376.

5. *Charlotte Western Democrat,* March 7, 1865. A virtually identical account of this incident referred to the horsemen as "A party of thirty-five Yankee foragers." See *Raleigh North Carolina Standard,* March 15, 1865.

6. *Charlotte Western Democrat,* March 21, 1865.

7. *Charlotte Western Democrat,* March 7, 1865. The term "galvanized Yankees" referred to Confederate prisoners or deserters who had joined the Union army.

8. J. G. de Roulhac Hamilton, ed., *The Correspondence of Jonathan Worth,* 2 vols. (Raleigh: North Carolina Historical Commission, 1909), 1:358–359.

9. Hamilton, *Correspondence of Jonathan Worth,* 1:360.

10. Sherman, *Memoirs,* 772; *Official Records . . . Armies,* ser. 1, 47, pt. 1:22, 689; Johnston, *Narrative,* 376; John G. Barrett, *Sherman's March through the Carolinas* (Chapel Hill: University of North Carolina Press, 1956), 106.

11. *Charlotte Western Democrat,* March 7, 1865.

12. *Charlotte Western Democrat,* March 7, 1865.

13. *Wadesboro Argus*, March 30, 1865.

14. Hamilton, *Correspondence of Jonathan Worth*, 1:361–363.

15. Sherman, *Memoirs*, 772–773; Johnston, *Narrative*, 376, 580–581; *Official Records . . . Armies*, ser. 1, 47, pt. 2:720; Barrett, *Sherman's March,* 107–108.

16. Sherman, *Memoirs*, 773–774; *Official Records . . . Armies*, ser. 1, 47, pt. 1:22–23; Barrett, *Sherman's March*, 108–109.

17. Sherman, *Memoirs*, 774.

18. Sherman, *Memoirs*, 774; Jacob D. Cox, *The March to the Sea: Franklin and Nashville* (New York: Charles Scribner's Sons, 1882; Wilmington, N.C.: Broadfoot Publishing Company, 1989), 181–183. See also Barrett, *Sherman's March*, 111–113, and John F. Marszalek, *Sherman: A Soldier's Passion for Order* (New York: Free Press, 1993), 327.

19. Cornelia Phillips Spencer, *The Last Ninety Days of the War in North-Carolina* (New York: Watchman Publishing Company, 1866), 62–63.

20. *Charlotte Western Democrat*, March 14, 1865.

21. *Wadesboro Argus*, March 30, 1865.

22. *Wadesboro Argus*, March 30, 1865.

23. *Wadesboro Argus*, March 30, 1865.

24. *Wadesboro Argus*, March 30, 1865; *Charlotte Western Democrat*, March 21, 1865; Spencer, *Last Ninety Days of the War*, 64. See also Mary L. Medley, *History of Anson County, North Carolina, 1750–1976* (Wadesboro: Anson County Historical Society, 1976), 118–123, and John M. Gibson, *Those 163 Days: A Southern Account of Sherman's March from Atlanta to Raleigh* (New York: Coward-McCann, 1961), 189–190.

25. E. B. Long, *The Civil War Day by Day: An Almanac, 1861–1865* (Garden City, N.J.: Doubleday and Company, 1971), 647; Robert E. Denney, *The Civil War Years: A Day-by-Day Chronicle of the Life of a Nation* (New York: Sterling Publishing Company, 1992), 542.

26. Denney, *The Civil War Years*, 542; George W. Pepper, *Personal Recollections of Sherman's Campaigns in Georgia and the Carolinas* (Zanesville, Ohio: Hugh Dunne, 1866), 358.

27. Clement Eaton, ed., "Diary of an Officer in Sherman's Army Marching through the Carolinas," *Journal of Southern History* 9 (May 1943): 247.

28. Pepper, *Personal Recollections of Sherman's Campaigns*, 358.

29. Pepper, *Personal Recollections of Sherman's Campaigns*, 358.

30. *Official Records . . . Armies*, ser. 1, 47, pt. 1:689.

31. Johnston, *Narrative*, 378.

32. Johnston, *Narrative*, 380; *Official Records . . . Armies*, ser. 1, 47, pt. 2:720; Barrett, *Sherman's March*, 108.

33. Barrett, *Sherman's March*, 113.

34. *Charlotte Western Democrat*, April 4, 1865.

35. *Official Records . . . Armies*, ser. 1, 47, pt. 1:885; *Charlotte Western Democrat*, April 4, 1865. See also Barrett, *Sherman's March*, 113–114.

36. Spencer, *Last Ninety Days of the War*, 63.

37. Medley, *History of Anson County*, 119.

38. *Charlotte Western Democrat*, March 14, 1865, quoting earlier issue of the *Salisbury Carolina Watchman*.

39. *Charlotte Western Democrat*, March 21, 1865.

40. *Charlotte Western Democrat*, March 21, 1865.

41. Johnston, *Narrative*, 380; Pepper, *Personal Recollections of Sherman's Campaigns*, 358, 372; Gibson, *Those 163 Days*, 189; David P. Conyngham, *Sherman's March Through the South* (New York: Sheldon and Company, 1865), 354.

42. *Wadesboro Argus*, March 30, 1865.

43. Katharine M. Jones, *When Sherman Came: Southern Women and the "Great March"* (Indianapolis: Bobbs-Merrill, 1964), 262–263.

44. Johnston, *Narrative*, 374–375.

45. *Official Records . . . Armies*, ser. 1, 47, pt. 2:1324.

46. Johnston, *Narrative*, 374–375.

47. *Salisbury Carolina Watchman*, March 7, 1865.

48. *Fayetteville Observer*, March 9, 1865.

49. Sherman, *Memoirs*, 774–775. See also *Official Records . . . Armies*, ser. 1, 47, pt. 1:861; Pepper, *Personal Recollections of Sherman's Campaigns*, 358; and Conyngham, *Sherman's March Through the South*, 354.

50. Barrett, *Sherman's March*, 117.

51. *Official Records . . . Armies*, ser. 1, 47, pt. 2:703–704.

52. *Official Records . . . Armies*, ser. 1, 47, pt. 1:4; Barrett, *Sherman's March*, 113; Long, *The Civil War Day by Day*, 648.

53. *Fayetteville Observer*, March 6, 1865, quoting the *Winston Sentinel* of March 3, 1865.

54. *Fayetteville Observer*, March 6, 1865.

55. Barrett, *Sherman's March*, 122.

56. George Ward Nichols, *The Story of the Great March from the Diary of a Staff Officer* (New York: Harper and Brothers, 1865; Williamstown, Mass.: Corner House Publishers, 1972), 217.

57. *Official Records . . . Armies*, ser. 1, 47, pt. 1:690.

58. Nichols, *Story of the Great March*, 217.

59. Nichols, *Story of the Great March*, 218. For Sherman's views on the refugee problem, see, for example, Sherman, *Memoirs*, 779–781.

60. Johnston, *Narrative*, 381–382; *Official Records . . . Armies*, ser. 1, 47, pt. 1:4, 690, 1130; Barrett, *Sherman's March*, 115.

61. Pepper, *Personal Recollections of Sherman's Campaigns*, 342.

62. *Official Records . . . Armies*, ser. 1, 47, pt. 2:719.

63. *Official Records . . . Armies*, ser. 1, 47, pt. 2:721. On the general distinctions drawn between North and South Carolina, see also Barrett, *Sherman's March*, 119–121, and Henry Steele Commager, ed., *The Blue and the Gray: The Story of the Civil War as Told by Participants*, 2 vols. (Indianapolis: Bobbs-Merrill, 1950), 2:959.

64. Johnston, *Narrative*, 378–379; John G. Barrett, *The Civil War in North Carolina* (Chapel Hill: University of North Carolina Press, 1963), 285–286.

65. *Official Records . . . Armies*, ser. 1, 47, pt. 2:1345, 1352. See also Barrett, *Sherman's March*, 122.

66. *Official Records . . . Armies*, ser. 1, 47, pt. 1:864.

67. *Official Records . . . Armies*, ser. 1, 47, pt. 1:690. See also Barrett, *Sherman's March*, 122.

68. Robert Underwood Johnson and Clarence Clough Buel, eds., *Battles and Leaders of the Civil War*, 4 vols. (New York: Century Company, 1884–1888; New York: Thomas Yoseloff, 1956), 4:677–678. See also Commager, *The Blue and the Gray*, 2:963.

69. *Official Records . . . Armies*, ser. 1, 47, pt. 2:720–721. See also Barrett, *Sherman's March*, 115.

70. *Charlotte Western Democrat*, March 7, 1865.

71. Sherman, *Memoirs*, 775; *Official Records . . . Armies*, ser. 1, 47, pt. 1:551, 861; Barrett, *Sherman's March*, 122–125; Jones, *When Sherman Came*, 264; Thomas Ward Osborn, *The Fiery Trail: A Union Officer's Account of Sherman's Last Campaigns*, ed. Richard Harwell and Philip N. Racine (Knoxville: University of Tennessee Press, 1986), 171.

72. Barrett, *Civil War in North Carolina*, 301; Nichols, *Story of the Great March*, 223; Eaton, "Diary of an Officer", 247–248.

73. Nichols, *Story of the Great March*, 222.

74. Nichols, *Story of the Great March*, 222.

75. *Official Records . . . Armies*, ser. 1, 47, pt. 2:728.

76. Sherman, *Memoirs*, 775.

77. Barrett, *Civil War in North Carolina*, 286–288.

78. Barrett, *Civil War in North Carolina*, 286–288.

79. Barrett, *Civil War in North Carolina*, 300n.

80. Barrett, *Civil War in North Carolina*, 302.

81. Conyngham, *Sherman's March Through the South*, 355. See also Barrett, *Sherman's March*, 137, n. 16, and Gibson, *Those 163 Days*, 194–195.

82. Sherman, *Memoirs*, 775.

83. *Official Records . . . Armies*, ser. 1, 47, pt. 1:551, pt. 2:728; Barrett, *Sherman's March*, 124–125; Pepper, *Personal Recollections of Sherman's Campaigns*, 372.

84. Johnston, *Narrative*, 380; Barrett, *Sherman's March*, 125–126.

85. Johnston, *Narrative*, 379; Barrett, *Sherman's March*, 288–289.

86. Barrett, *Sherman's March*, 124.

87. Barrett, *Civil War in North Carolina*, 302n.

88. Gibson, *Those 163 Days*, 196.

89. *Raeford News-Journal*, June 20, 1930.

90. *Raeford News-Journal*, June 20, 1930.

91. Jones, *When Sherman Came*, 259.

92. Jones, *When Sherman Came*, 260.

93. Jones, *When Sherman Came*, 260.

94. Barrett, *Sherman's March*, 124–125.

95. Barrett, *Sherman's March*, 124–125.

96. Hamilton, *Correspondence of Jonathan Worth*, 1:364.

97. Barrett, *Sherman's March*, 130–131; Sherman, *Memoirs*, 775; Pepper, *Personal Recollections of Sherman's Campaigns*, 372; *Official Records . . . Armies*, ser. 1, 47, pt. 1:551; Osborn, *The Fiery Trail*, 173.

98. Barrett, *Sherman's March*, 126–130; Sherman, *Memoirs*, 776; Johnston, *Narrative*, 380–381; *Official Records . . . Armies*, ser. 1, 47, pt. 1:861–862, 1130; Gibson, *Those 163 Days*, 196–200.

99. *Official Records . . . Armies*, ser. 1, 47, pt. 2:760–761. See also ser. 1, 47, pt. 2:783, and Barrett, *Sherman's March*, 119–121.

100. Barrett, *Civil War in North Carolina*, 289–290; Johnston, *Narrative*, 379–380.

101. Johnston, *Narrative*, 381; Osborn, *The Fiery Trail*, 179.

102. Jones, *When Sherman Came*, 264–265.

103. *Official Records . . . Armies*, ser. 1, 47, pt. 2:382. See also Barrett, *Sherman's March*, 130.

104. This letter of March 10 to the editor of the *Raleigh Daily Conservative* was subsequently published in the *Charlotte Western Democrat* on March 21, 1865.

105. Sherman, *Memoirs*, 775–777; Johnston, *Narrative*, 382, 582; Barrett, *Sherman's March*, 132–133; Gibson, *Those 163 Days*, 201–202.

106. Barrett, *Sherman's March*, 132–134; *Official Records . . . Armies*, ser. 1, 1, pt. 1:551; Sherman, *Memoirs*, 775–777; Pepper, *Personal Recollections of Sherman's Campaigns*, 372; Gibson, *Those 163 Days*, 202.

107. Sherman, *Memoirs*, 777; *Official Records . . . Armies*, ser. 1, 47, pt. 2:779. See also Barrett, *Sherman's March*, 135.

108. *Official Records . . . Armies*, ser. 1, 47, pt. 2:779.

109. *Official Records . . . Armies*, ser. 1, 47, pt. 2:779.

110. Johnston, *Narrative*, 382; Sherman, *Memoirs*, 775–776.

111. Barrett, *Sherman's March*, 143–144; Spencer, *Last Ninety Days of the War*, 50–51.

112. Jones, *When Sherman Came*, 273–274.

113. Spencer, *Last Ninety Days of the War*, 50.

114. *Official Records . . . Armies*, ser. 1, 47, pt. 1:551.

115. Pepper, *Personal Recollections of Sherman's Campaigns*, 343.

116. Jones, *When Sherman Came*, 266.

117. Jones, *When Sherman Came*, 266–267.

118. Jones, *When Sherman Came*, 277–279.

119. Jones, *When Sherman Came*, 272.

120. See, for example, Spencer, *Last Ninety Days of the War*, 66–68; Barrett, *Sherman's March*, 144–145; Hamilton, *Correspondence of Jonathan Worth*, 1:367–368; and Gibson, *Those 163 Days*, 203–204.

121. Barrett, *Sherman's March*, 137, n. 20.

122. Nichols, *Story of the Great March*, 239.

123. *Official Records . . . Armies*, ser. 1, 47, pt. 2:782.

124. Sherman, *Memoirs*, 777.

125. Sherman, *Memoirs*, 781.

126. Sherman, *Memoirs*, 778–780.

127. Barrett, *Civil War in North Carolina*, 315.

128. Hamilton, *Correspondence of Jonathan Worth*, 1:367–368.

129. Hamilton, *Correspondence of Jonathan Worth*, 1:365.

130. Long, *The Civil War Day by Day*, 651.

131. Sherman, *Memoirs*, 781; Osborn, *The Fiery Trail*, 181; Gibson, *Those 163 Days*, 207; Denney, *The Civil War Years*, 546.

132. *Official Records . . . Armies*, ser. 1, 47, pt. 2:807.

133. Nichols, *Story of the Great March*, 252.

134. F. Y. Hedley, *Marching through Georgia: Pen-Pictures of Every-Day Life in General Sherman's Army* (Chicago: R. R. Donelley and Sons, 1887), 401–405; Glatthaar, *March to the Sea and Beyond*, 60–62.

135. *Official Records . . . Armies*, ser. 1, 47, pt. 1:1130; Johnston, *Narrative*, 382.

136. *Official Records . . . Armies*, ser. 1, 47, pt. 1:23.

137. *Official Records . . . Armies*, ser. 1, 47, pt. 1:23. See also Barrett, *Sherman's March*, 142–143. The ruins of the arsenal were burned the following day.

138. Eaton, "Diary of An Officer," 248.

139. Barrett, *Sherman's March*, 146, n. 63.

140. Barrett, *Civil War in North Carolina*, 315.

141. Gibson, *Those 163 Days*, 204.

142. Jones, *When Sherman Came*, 268.

143. Spencer, *Last Ninety Days of the War*, 66–67.

144. Spencer, *Last Ninety Days of the War*, 66–67.

145. Spencer, *Last Ninety Days of the War*, 67, 67n. Among the dwellings burned near Fayetteville "in one neighborhood" were those of C. T. Haigh, J. C. Haigh, Archibald Graham, and W. T. Horne.

146. Spencer, *Last Ninety Days of the War*, 67–68, 68 n. The four men hanged were J. P. McLean, W. T. Horne, Jesse Hawley, and Alexander McArthur. The man killed in his home was John Waddell. See also Barrett, *Sherman's March*, 144–145, and the *Charlotte Western Democrat*, March 28, 1865.

147. *Charlotte Western Democrat*, March 21, 1865, reprinted from the *Raleigh Daily Conservative* of March 15, 1865.

148. Sherman, *Memoirs*, 781–782; *Official Records . . . Armies*, ser. 1, 47, pt. 1:551; Barrett, *Sherman's March*, 147.

149. *Official Records . . . Armies*, ser. 1, 47, pt. 1:4, 1130; Johnston, *Narrative*, 382.

150. Sherman, *Memoirs*, 781–782.

151. Sherman, *Memoirs*, 781–782; Osborn, *The Fiery Trail*, 183.

152. Sherman, *Memoirs*, 782; Barrett, *Sherman's March*, 137, 137 n. 20; Osborn, *The Fiery Trail*, 183.

153. *Charlotte Western Democrat*, March 28, 1865.

154. Barrett, *Civil War in North Carolina*, 290n.

155. *Official Records . . . Armies*, ser. 1, 47, pt. 1:23; Barrett, *Sherman's March*, 149.

156. Barrett, *Civil War in North Carolina*, 315.

157. Jones, *When Sherman Came*, 285.

158. Sherman, *Memoirs*, 781; *Official Records . . . Armies*, ser. 1, 47, pt. 1:23.

159. Eaton, "Diary of an Officer," 248; John A. Oates, *The Story of Fayetteville and the Upper Cape Fear* (Charlotte: Dowd Press, 1950), 412.

160. Jones, *When Sherman Came*, 281.

161. Jones, *When Sherman Came*, 269–270.

162. Barrett, *Sherman's March*, 142; *Charlotte Western Democrat*, March 28, 1865.

163. *Official Records . . . Armies*, ser. 1, 47, pt. 1:551. See also Barrett, *Sherman's March*, 141.

164. Barrett, *Sherman's March*, 141.

165. Barrett, *Sherman's March*, 141, 146.

166. *Charlotte Western Democrat*, March 28, 1865, reprinted from *Hillsborough Recorder* of March 22, 1865.

167. Eaton, "Diary of an Officer," 248.

168. Jones, *When Sherman Came*, 281–283.

PART 2

March 15–April 11, 1865

March 15 (Wednesday)

After he left Fayetteville, Sherman planned to capture Goldsboro and its railroad connections. The march proceeded with his army divided as before, the left wing composed of the Fourteenth and Twentieth Corps and accompanied by Gen. Judson Kilpatrick's cavalry and the right wing consisting of the Fifteenth and Seventeenth Corps. Sherman accompanied Gen. Henry W. Slocum and the Fourteenth Corps. Heavy rains impeded the march. According to Samuel Toombs of the Thirteenth Regiment of New Jersey Volunteers, it was a "stormy day with fierce lightning, and the road a perfect sea of mud."[1]

Sherman ordered Kilpatrick to move his cavalry up the plank road to and beyond Averasboro on the east bank of the Cape Fear. Four divisions of the left wing, with as few wagons as possible, were to follow. The remaining two divisions were to escort the rest of the supply train along a shorter and more direct route to Goldsboro. Sherman instructed Gen. O. O. Howard to send the supply trains well to the right of the general line of march in the direction of Faison's Depot. Sherman also directed Howard to hold four divisions of the right wing in readiness to go to the aid of the left wing if it became necessary.[2]

Confederate general Joseph E. Johnston's primary purpose in North Carolina was to isolate and strike one of Sherman's columns on the move. With his forces widely scattered, Johnston selected Smithfield as a concentration point for the different commands. While he consolidated his troops, Johnston ordered Gen. William J. Hardee and his cavalry to parallel Sherman's route so to be constantly in a position to force delaying action.[3]

Hardee established a position about five or six miles south of Averasboro near Smith's Mill (also called Smithville locally), while Gen. Joseph Wheeler's detachment of the cavalry moved ahead to slow the advance guard of Sherman's left wing. Union general Kilpatrick's cavalry, preceding the left wing on the Raleigh road, slowly pushed Wheeler back. Meanwhile, Hardee deployed for

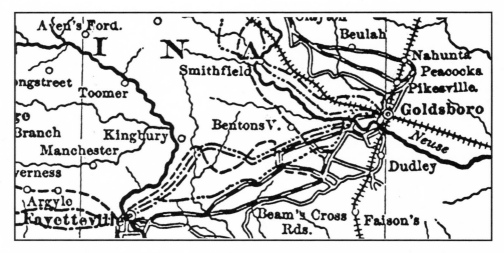

Between March 15 and April 11, 1865, Sherman's forces marched through this portion of North Carolina. Detail of map from Force, *General Sherman*, opposite 295.

battle. He ordered Col. Alfred Moore Rhett's brigade into position in rear of an open field on the right of the road, erected breastworks that extended about seven miles from the Black River to the Cape Fear, and established a skirmish line a few hundred yards in front.[4]

Around three o'clock in the afternoon Kilpatrick's unit, with the Ninth Michigan Cavalry in advance, struck the Confederate skirmish line. The rebels offered some "pretty stubborn resistance," and the fighting continued until dark. Kilpatrick was forced to halt his advance, and his men threw up rail barricades to help ward off the Confederates until reinforcements could arrive.[5]

Sherman, still with the Fourteenth Corps, took refuge for the night in an old cooper's shop, where he received Col. Alfred Rhett (of a distinguished South Carolina family and a former commander of Fort Sumter), a prisoner whom Kilpatrick's men had captured in the day's skirmish.[6]

March 16 (Thursday)

Skirmishing resumed about six o'clock in the morning. General Sherman ordered General Slocum to take part of the Twentieth Corps to aid Kilpatrick. Bad weather and equally bad roads slowed the reinforcements, and they did not reach the battle area until 10:00 A.M. They arrived just in time to turn the tide of battle in favor of the Union forces. Although unable to overrun the Confederate breastworks, they did force Hardee to make a strategic retreat. According to Jessie S. Smith, a local resident, "Those [Confederates] who escaped were so closely pressed that they were unable to bury their dead, so the enemy placed the bodies in hastily dug graves." [The bodies were later disinterred and removed to Chicora Cemetery.][7]

Although the contest has been called the Battle of Averasboro, in strict military terms it should not be described in that manner. It was a delaying action, a skirmish, although an intense one. A participant on the Union side commented that "The musketry fire often rose nearly to the dignity of a battle." Losses for the Federals included 95 killed, 533 wounded, and 54 missing. Total Confederate losses were put at 865.[8] The battlefield was located on the lands of John Smith, whose home, Oak Grove, became a Confederate hospital. Women in the neighborhood assisted in bringing the wounded and dying to the house, in which "The groans of the dying and the complaints of those undergoing amputation was horrible."[9]

During the fighting, the home of Farquhard Smith was confiscated and used as Federal headquarters. Smith had sent eight sons into Confederate service, and when General Slocum asked to meet the lady of the house, inasmuch as he was a relative of Mrs. Smith, her husband replied, "When you crossed the Mason and Dixon line, all ties of blood are lost." The home of William Smith served as a Federal hospital. The parlor was converted into an operating room and the piano used as an operating table. Federal soldiers who died there were initially buried in the garden but later moved to the Federal cemetery in Raleigh.[10]

Janie Smith, whose home was in the community surrounding the battlefield, left a negative impression of the Union soldiers. She wrote: "They left no living thing in Smithville [the community south of Averasboro] but people, and one old hen who played sick, thus saving her neck but losing her biddies."[11] Jessie S. Smith, a relative of Janie, echoed Janie's observations: "Those were poverty days for the community. First Johnston's army had passed through taking the necessary supplies for our men, and then came Sherman's army pillaging everywhere."[12] A more positive picture, however, emerged from the battlefield itself. Before the Union troops departed, Federal surgeons performed necessary operations on wounded Confederates, and Sherman himself visited one of the makeshift hospitals where the surgeons were performing such service.[13]

Sherman's memoirs reveal further the corruptive influence of war upon the manners and humanity of those who fought. During the Battle of Averasboro a man on foot, without shoes or coat and his head bandaged in a handkerchief, approached Sherman. The man said he was Captain Duncan and that he had been captured by Wade Hampton in Fayetteville but later escaped. He explained that when Hampton's men had made him "get out of his coat, hat, and shoes," which they appropriated to themselves, Hampton watched and did nothing. When Duncan appealed to Hampton for protection as an officer, Hampton replied with a curse. Sherman placed Duncan in Kilpatrick's unit, and the Union commander subsequently heard that Kilpatrick had forced the captured Confederate Colonel Rhett (see above) to march on foot the rest of the way to Goldsboro in retaliation for the alleged treatment of Captain Duncan. Sherman denied any personal involvement or prior knowledge of Kilpatrick's action.[14]

Meanwhile, citizens elsewhere in North Carolina were having problems with deserters and the Confederate army itself. Mrs. Elvira Worth Jackson of Asheboro wrote to Mrs. Jonathan Worth:

We have had more peaceable times with the deserters since you left. I hear of no robbing being commited since these [Confederate] troops came in, and a large number of cavalry and wagons have passed here on their way to Raleigh. You ought to have seen us hiding meat, corn, etc. the other day. We heard that 4000 cavalry were to pass here and we knew if they did we would be eaten out so we went to hiding hay and provisions. Fortunately for us the cavalry turned off and went by Thomasville.[15]

S. S. Jackson, husband of Elvira Worth Jackson, wrote to Jonathan Worth the same day: "A wagon train and cavalry are continuously passing through this place and the neighborhood on their way to Raleigh, as they say, pressing horses, forage, etc."[16]

March 17 (Friday)

At 6:40 A.M. Wheeler reported to General Hardee that "The prisoner captured this morning states that their Army are [sic] going to Goldsboro and not to Raleigh." At 1:00 P.M. Hardee sent General Johnston a dispatch stating that he was relocating to Elevation (about halfway between Averasboro and Smithfield) and that preliminary intelligence indicated that Sherman was not moving toward Raleigh. A second dispatch at 2:50 P.M. speculated that Sherman's destination was Goldsboro.[17] Hardee's retreat had left 108 unburied dead on the field and 68 severely wounded for the Union surgeons to care for. The surgeons carefully dressed the wounds of the survivors and left them with as much medicine as could be spared, and a commissary officer left a few days' supply of food. A captured Confederate officer and several other prisoners were placed in charge of their unfortunate comrades.[18]

Col. S. D. Pool, Confederate commander at Goldsboro, received from Assistant Adjutant General John B. Sale a message that General Johnston planned to defend Goldsboro. To that end, Capt. William H. James, an assistant engineer, was directed to secure black labor and build a line of entrenchments near that city.[19] Kilpatrick crossed the Black River and moved out on the Smithfield road to the left and front of the Fourteenth and Twentieth Corps (left wing) on the direct route to Goldsboro. The Seventeenth Corps took the road to Clinton. When within six miles of that place, Gen. Frank P. Blair Jr. sent the Ninth Illinois Mounted Infantry forward to cover the refugee train moving from Fayetteville to Wilmington, as ordered by Sherman. General Terry's forces were marching north from Wilmington for the rendezvous at Goldsboro.[20]

March 18 (Saturday)

At daybreak, Johnston received a message from General Hampton that Sherman was marching for Goldsboro. Johnston ordered troops at Smithfield and Elevation to Bentonville to prepare for battle with Sherman's left wing. Hampton threw light entrenchments across the road between the Federal camp and the proposed field of battle to delay the Union march until Hardee's Corps could arrive from Elevation.[21]

Sherman continued to travel with General Slocum's column of the left wing. At 2:00 P.M. he sent a dispatch to General Howard stating that he thought the enemy was concentrated around Smithfield and that he expected Johnston to try to prevent the Union army from reaching Goldsboro. Later that day he sent a second dispatch, based largely on a report from Kilpatrick, saying that he thought Johnston was nearer Raleigh. He ordered Howard to "make a break into Goldsborough from the South, and let your scouts strike out for Schofield at Kinston, though I hope to meet him at Goldsborough."[22]

The Fourteenth Corps moved toward Goldsboro with Brig. Gen. James D. Morgan's division in the lead. Confederate general Wade Hampton's cavalry unit kept up a series of hit-and-run tactics. In the heavily wooded area, Federals found numerous turpentine stills and burned them, sending up dense columns of black smoke, which gave the Confederates the precise location of the Union advance. Confederate cavalry dug in at Bushy Swamp and opened artillery fire that halted the Union march for the night.[23] Meanwhile, the Twentieth Corps of the left wing had moved only twelve miles after crossing Black River because of the mud and mire. It encamped for the night of the eighteenth at Lee's plantation, nearly eight miles in the rear of the Fourteenth Corps. The right wing moved on somewhat parallel roads to the south. Logan's Fifteenth Corps was six miles south of Slocum's Fourteenth Corps on the night of March 18. The Seventeenth Corps stopped in the vicinity of Troublefield's Store. Sherman, who had been traveling with the Fourteenth Corps, interpreted the dispatches of this day to mean that the danger of attack had passed. During the night, he crossed overland to join General Howard's column of the right wing so as to be nearer to a juncture with Schofield and Terry, who were approaching Goldsboro from the east and south.[24]

On the night of the eighteenth, General Hampton gave General Johnston all information on the positions of Federal troops and recommended ground near the Goldsboro road and about two miles south of Bentonville as favorable for battle. Even with the Twentieth Corps well in the rear, the troops of Slocum's Fourteenth Corps and Kilpatrick's cavalry numbered about thirty thousand, compared to Johnston's entire army of about twenty thousand.[25]

March 19 (Sunday)

The foragers of the Fourteenth Corps, as usual, proceeded in advance of the main body. They encountered and engaged the pickets set up by Hampton, but word of a major Confederate buildup was not relayed to Slocum or Sherman. The Federal left wing began its march at 7:00 A.M., with the First Division of the Fourteenth Corps in the lead. The sudden appearance of Johnston's entire command took them by surprise. The Battle at Bentonville had begun, and for a few hours the Confederate forces held the advantage. Late in the afternoon the advance units of the Twentieth Corps reached the battle area and stemmed the forward movements of Johnston's troops. Sherman, learning that he had been deceived as to Johnston's actual location and that the Confederate general threatened to destroy a large segment of his army, ordered General Logan to take the Fifteenth Corps immediately to assist Slocum. The Seventeenth Corps was to follow as soon as possible.[26]

When a staff officer from the advance guard returned to the main body of the Fourteenth Corps to report the initiation of action and to bring reinforcements, soldiers of the Twenty-second Wisconsin asked him how the fighting had begun. He replied:

> Them damned bummers of ours started out this morning before daylight, as thay [sic] always do, to get ahead of the soldiers. Before we had our breakfast, we knew they'd run against a snag for we could hear the firing. Before we were through eating, back came one of them, hellaty scoot, his horse laying down to it when he rode into camp, and he says, "Hurry up boys, and give us some help, for the rebs don't drive worth a darn today!" And that's the way it commenced, boys.[27]

March 20 (Monday)

Less fighting took place on this day than on the nineteenth. By noon the Fifteenth Corps arrived on the scene, and the rest of the day was spent mostly in tactical maneuvering, with an occasional skirmish. General Howard brought more reinforcements from the right wing and reached the battlefield at 4:00 P.M.[28]

Meanwhile, Sherman's foragers, well in advance of the main columns, made their first appearance at Everettsville, a community a few miles south of Goldsboro. One of the homes they approached was that of Elizabeth Collier, who left the following account:

> They asked for flour and seeing that we were disposed not to give it, made a rush in the house—the cowardly creature even pointed his gun at us—*helpless* women. Looking out we soon found that poor little Everettsville was filled with Yankees and they were plundering the houses. After a while we succeeded in getting a "Safe guard," and for a week we got along comparatively well. But in the meantime everything out doors was destroyed—all provisions taken—fences knocked down—*horses, cows, carriages and buggies stolen* and everything else the wretches could lay their hands on—even to the *servants* clothes.[29]

The *Daily Progress* of Raleigh reported on the conduct of Wheeler's Confederate cavalry as it passed through the capital on the way to Bentonville:

> We have no doubt but much unjust abuse has been heaped on the cavalry under the command of Gen. Wheeler, and that much of the marauding and plundering charged to them has been perpetrated by others. Several of them have been at the house of the Editor of this paper for nearly a week past, and we can with truth say that we have never seen a more orderly or well behaved set of men. Their deportment has been that of perfect gentlemen, and if these be a fair specimen of the corps, no one but Yankees need be afraid of them.[30]

Southerners, however, did contribute to the problems of local residents. Gen. Joseph R. Hawley, Union commander at Wilmington District Headquarters, wrote to Lt. Col. J. A. Campbell: "Stray marauders annoy the inhabitants in all the regions about us, but more particularly in Bladen and Brunswick Counties. In those districts are many rebel deserters, in some instances organized as companies. They subsist on the inhabitants, chiefly directing their attention to citizens of strong rebel proclivities, and especially against enrolling officers &c. . . . "[31]

March 21 (Tuesday)

Sherman now had his entire army in the field at Bentonville. Confederate resistance became less effective. Johnston, outnumbered in manpower by nearly four to one, in danger of having his only line of retreat cut by flanking Union forces, and learning that Union general Schofield had taken Goldsboro, withdrew his troops during the night. Casualties for the North totaled more than fifteen hundred and for the South more than twenty-six hundred, many of whom were captured. All Confederate wounded that could withstand transportation were removed from the battlefield. Johnston ordered his army to cross Mill Creek by way of the bridge at Bentonville before daybreak of the twenty-second. Wheeler's cavalry fought a rearguard action, preventing Federals from crossing the bridge in immediate pursuit.[32]

In his diary, George Ward Nichols, one of Sherman's staff officers, commented on the Confederate resistance at Bentonville: "For some reason which does not yet appear, the Rebels contest every foot of ground with extraordinary pertinacity; more tenaciously than the occasion seems to require."[33]

The Twentieth Corps of Sherman's army crossed the Neuse River south of the main scene of battle and resumed the march toward Goldsboro. In doing so, the men passed another Union corps stationed on the east side and noted that it included a Negro regiment.[34]

As the fighting at Bentonville entered its final day, General Schofield's army had begun the last leg of its march to Goldsboro with the Ninth New Jersey Volunteers in the lead. Though Confederate resistance was expected at any time, none was encountered until the Ninth came into Webbtown, a few miles from the county seat. There a force of Confederate infantry checked the Union cavalry advance but retreated when the full body of the Ninth rushed the field.[35]

Col. S. D. Pool, the Confederate commander in Goldsboro, decided to evacuate the town. Troops began to pull out at 4:00 P.M. after setting fire to the cotton in storage.[36] It was left to Mayor James H. Privett to surrender the town. The following account came from John R. Morris and appeared in the *Goldsboro Daily Argus*, November 9, 1890:

> Privett, unarmed and carrying a white flag rode out beyond Webbtown to meet the Union officers with an offer of surrender. He was met by a dozen soldiers of the advance guard who surrounded him, yelling curses. One was reported to have grabbed his horse in an attempt to break its neck. Privett held the white flag and calmly told the mob, "I am the mayor of Goldsboro" and demanded to meet the commanding officer. Before they could harm Mayor Privett, a group of Union soldiers "martial in appearance and gentlemanly in

address" arrived and saluted the mayor. These were cavalrymen of the Ninth New Jersey Regiment who were commissioned to secure the town for the officers that followed.

Mayor Privett told the officers who he was and that he wanted to surrender the town. The officers accepted, but warned him that Goldsboro was at their mercy. Mayor Privett acknowledged that and said, "before you march into town, assure me protection for property, women and children." In return for such a pledge, the people of Goldsboro offered to share their homes. The officers withdrew and later returned to tell Privett that Colonel Stewart, the commanding officer, had agreed to the requests.[37]

Schofield promptly deployed the Ninth, and within half an hour after its entry into the town was patrolling the streets. Dr. Gillette, a physician/surgeon accompanying the Ninth New Jersey, immediately sought a building in which to care for the sick and wounded being brought along in wagons. He selected a large brick structure previously used as a seminary for young ladies.[38] A short time later General Schofield rode into an orderly town still filled with the smell of burning cotton.

According to Nichols, it was a common sight to see Confederates destroy their own facilities in the path of Union march: "Upon our approach from Savannah to Goldsboro, hundreds of bridges and railways were burned by the Rebel military in spite of protests and prayers of the local inhabitants." He added that such burnings often occurred from a petty feeling of spite rather than military necessity.[39] Nichols also left a vivid description of the destruction caused by the Union army, which he saw as a sorrowful but not unexpected aspect of war:

Day by day our [Union] legions of armed men surged over the land, destroying its substance. Cattle were gathered into increasing droves; fresh horses taken to replace the lame and feeble animals; rich graneries and store-houses stripped of corn, fodder, meal, and flour; cotton-gins, presses factories, and mills were burned to the ground; on every side, the head, centre, and rear of our column might be traced by columns of smoke by day and the glare of fires by night. Injury to private dwellings was forbidden, and food for present necessities was often left for the women and children, but in all the length and breadth of that broad pathway, the burning hand of war pressed heavily, blasting and withering where it fell. It was the penalty of rebellion.[40]

Such destruction prompted Catherine Ann Devereux Edmondston of Halifax County to record in her diary the contention that Sherman's men were "murderous scoundrels." She added: "I hope for better things. Johnston will defeat Sherman, perhaps kill him or shoot off his other leg & compel him to retreat & we will be saved the miseries of having our whole county overrun by the bloodthirsty harpies. Johnston, I am confident will be victorious, yet, nevertheless, we live in a state of anxious excitement pitiable to witness."[41]

March 22 (Wednesday)

Sherman directed General Howard and Kilpatrick's cavalry to remain at Bentonville to bury the dead and remove the wounded. He then rode to Cox's Bridge to meet General Terry, who was en route from Wilmington to Goldsboro.[42] At ten o'clock in the morning Sherman ordered Kilpatrick to continue to gather food and forage. "I claim," he wrote, "the absolute right to all property lying south of our route of march, and care not how close you pinch the inhabitants, if it be done without pillage of mere household goods and apparel of women."[43] Some of the Confederate soldiers at Bentonville deserted after the battle and went to Bladen, Columbus, and Brunswick Counties to join the band of renegades raiding the countryside in that region.[44]

T. M. Paysinger, Confederate sergeant of scouts, wrote to Generals Lafayette McLaws and William J. Hardee that parts of the Twenty-Fourth and Twenty-Fifth Corps under Union general Schofield were crossing the Neuse River at Cox's Bridge about ten miles above Goldsboro and that two divisions of that group were Negroes.[45]

In Goldsboro, a large freight warehouse and a storehouse near the depot were destroyed by fire. A Union soldier of the Ninth New Jersey wrote in his diary that it was the work of "vindictive citizens who had been too cowardly to fire a gun in defense of the place."[46] Colonel Pool wrote to Col. J. B. Sale about abandoning Goldsboro: "I evacuated Goldsborough at 4 p.m. yesterday; reached here [Wilson] at 11 o'clock today. Large Yankee force in Goldsborough. . . . Everything was destroyed that could not be brought off."[47] General Schofield issued a public proclamation to the people of Goldsboro. All citizens who wished to have guard protection for their houses could get one by applying to the provost marshal's office located in Dr. John Davis's residence.[48]

March 23 (Thursday)

Generals Sherman and Terry rode into Goldsboro, where they met General Schofield, who had arrived two days earlier. About noon the left wing of the Union army reached Goldsboro. The right wing arrived a few hours later. Sherman had consolidated his army of approximately one hundred thousand men in eastern North Carolina. The task now was to re-equip the army after its long march.[49]

Schofield had chosen the E. B. Borden residence at 111 South George Street as his headquarters and selected the residence of Richard Washington at 219 South Center Street for General Sherman. The other generals were housed as follows: O. O. Howard in the home of W. T. Dortch on North William Street; Jacob D. Cox in the Everitt-Arrington House at 301 North George Street; Frank P. Blair Jr. at Mrs. Harriet B. Dewey's dwelling on the southeast corner of Walnut and James Streets; John A. Logan in part of J. C. Slocumb's home at Walnut and Slocumb Streets; Henry W. Slocumb (no relation to J. C.) with a Mrs. Alford, who lived at the southeast corner of Ash and James Streets; B. F. Baker in Dr. John D. Spicer's home at 207 South Center Street; and George H. Gordon as the guest of Jesse J. Baker (no relation to the Union general) at 314 South William Street.[50]

Shortly after the generals were situated, the Union troops lined up to pass in review, the Fourteenth Corps leading the way. In his diary, an Indiana soldier described the troops' appearance:

We marched in platoons, and I doubt if at any time the troops of the rebel army were more ragged than we. Probably one man in a dozen had a full set of clothes, but even this suit was patched or full of holes. . . . Many were bareheaded or had a handkerchief tied around their head. Many had on hats they had found in the houses along the line of march, an old worn out affair in every instance—tall crushed silk hats, some revolutionary styles, many without tops, caps so holey that the hair was sticking out, brimless hats, brimless caps, hats mostly brim.

Many men had no coats or wore buttonless blouses, and being without shirts their naked chests protruded. Many a coat had no sleeves, or one only, the sleeves having been used to patch the seat or knees of the trousers. . . . Generally both legs of the trousers were off nearly to the knees, though now and then a man more fortunate had only one leg exposed. Socks had disappeared weeks before, and many a shoeless patriot kept step with a half-shod comrade. But the men who had cut off the tails of their dress coats "to stop a hole to keep the wind away" though bronzed and weather beaten, marched by General Sherman with heads up.[51]

A correspondent for the *New York Tribune* penned this description of the troops:

Here came men strutting in mimic dignity in an old swallowtailed coat, with plug hats, the tops knocked in; there a group in seedy coats and pants of Rebel grey, with arms and legs protruding beyond all semblance of fit or fashion; short jackets, long tailed surcoats, and coats of every cast with broadtails, narrow tails, no tails at all—all of them most antiquated styles. Some wore women's bonnets, or young ladies hats with streamers or faded ribbons floating fantastically in the wind.

The procession of vehicles and animals was of the most grotesque description. There were donkeys large and small, almost smothered under burdens of turkeys, geese and other kinds of poultry, ox carts, skinny horses pulling in the fills of some parish doctors old sulkies, farm wagons and buggies, hacks, chaises, rockaways, aristocratic and family carriages, all filled with plunder and provisions.

There was bacon, ham, potatoes, flour, pork, sorghum, and freshly slaughtered pigs, sheep, and poultry dangling from saddle tree and wagon, enough, one would suppose, to feed the army for a fortnight.[52]

Some of the Negroes of Goldsboro, when they saw the soot-begrimed faces of those ragged soldiers, remarked that they were whiter than the soldiers.[53] Gen. Manning F. Force called the review a "sorry sight," and another officer noted that "nearly every soldier had some token of the march on his bayonet from a pig to a potato." Sherman is said to have remarked almost apologetically to General Schofield: "They don't march very well, but they will fight."[54] A correspondent for the *New York World* observed an uneasiness exhibited in the general's mannerisms:

Sherman acts as if he would rather be engaged in another kind of business . . . he seems all the while to be wishing it was over. While the troops are going by he must be carrying on a conversation or smoking or fidgeting in some way or other. . . . Very often he looks up just in time to snatch off his hat . . . and the way he puts that hat on again! With a jerk and a drag and a jam as if it were the most objectionable hat in the world and he was especially entitled to entertain an implacable grudge against it.[55]

After a number of the troops had passed, Sherman realized that nothing positive was being accomplished by the review and called it to a halt.

Confederate troops retreated westward, where the advance units passed through Chapel Hill. David L. Swain, president of the University of North Carolina, commented on their presence in a letter to William A. Graham: "They demean themselves quietly, not withstanding one of our citizens sends out to them small quantities of whiskey. Some 50 mounted men and a long wagon train are passing as I write. . . . Some of my neighbors have been constrained to furnish inconvenient supplies of corn, as well as long forage, and we will all breathe more freely when it shall be ascertained that they are all through."[56]

March 24 (Friday)

Kilpatrick's cavalry moved to Mount Olive, and General Terry took his troops to Faison's Depot. Still, the sheer number of Union troops in Goldsboro presented housing problems. In a letter to General Grant, Sherman declared his intent to "push all remaining families in Goldsboro out to Raleigh or Wilmington as Union troops will need every house in town."[57]

In the afternoon, the first of Kilpatrick's force, the Ninth Pennsylvania Cavalry, arrived in Mount Olive. Kilpatrick sent this message to Sherman: "The country is full of forage. General [Smith D.] Atkins, with his brigade, is at Clinton, gathering in supplies from the country to bring to this point [Mount Olive]. I have three successful mills in operation; intend to grind corn in the cob for my animals; corn meal and flour for my men."[58]

A diarist from the Ninth New Jersey described an early encounter with some of Sherman's army:

Sherman's westerners, when they came into the town, wanted to paint things red, but the orders and discipline of the men of the Ninth New Jersey did not permit conduct of this character, whereupon the Jerseymen were twitted as "white-gloved soldiers." A number of "bummers," having a contempt for men whose hands were covered with white gloves, got into trouble and the lock-up by attempting to do as they pleased—the Jerseymen having seen too much service and knowing their duty too well to permit themselves to be imposed upon, even by those heroes who had been on a picknicking march from "Atlanta to the sea."[59]

The *Western Sentinel* of Winston commented that "all along their line of march, the Federals stole horses, mules, cattle, slaves, food supplies, cotton, and personal provisions from the homes of the people."[60] The foraging report of the Third Division of the Seventeenth Corps alone tends to support the *Sentinel*'s claim:

Sweet potatoes, lbs.	60,000
Corn meal, lbs.	100,000
Cured meat, lbs.	200,000
Molasses, galls.	150
Sugar, bbls.	8
Salt, bbls.	15
Coffee, bbls.	1
Corn, bush.	7,000
Horses (captured)	350
Mules (captured)	230
Horses (killed)	180
Mules (killed)	130[61]

The commander of the Third Division defended the foraging activities: "But in a sparsely settled region, where towns are few and small and scantily supplied, and provisions are mainly found on scattered plantations, there is no alternative [such as requisition]; there is no means of obtaining supplies but by direct seizure."[62]

Some soldiers expanded the definition to include "everything on foot and wing, all things of the earth and air," and most all personal items were considered to be "contrabands of war." The term "bummer" was coined after the Atlanta campaign in 1864. In the Southern mind, the activities of Sherman's "bummers" in the march from Savannah to Raleigh came to personify outrageous pillaging.[63] Sherman's aide-de-camp, George Ward Nichols, described the arrival of the "bummers" in Goldsboro, which he termed "funny": "They rode into Goldsborough mounted upon all sorts of animals and in every description of costume. Hundreds of wagons, carts, buggies, barouches, hacks, wheel barrows, and all sorts of vehicles were loaded with bacon, meal, corn, oats, and fodder all gathered in the rich country through which they had marched during the day."[64]

Union general James D. Morgan did not hold as high an opinion of the "bummers." He acknowledged the value of foragers to the success of Sherman's campaign, but added:

> I regret that I have to except anyone from praise and credit, but I have some men in my command . . . who have mistaken the name and meaning of the term foragers, and have become under that name highwaymen, with all of the cruelty and ferocity and none of their courage; their victims are usually old men, women, and children, and the Negroes whom they rob and maltreat without mercy, firing dwellings, and outhouses even when filled with grain that the army needs, and sometimes endangering the trains by the universal firing of fences. These men are a disgrace to the name of soldier and the country. I desire to place upon record my detestation and abhorrence of their acts.[65]

Thomas C. Fuller, who lived near Fayetteville, verified General Morgan's account of actions by undisciplined Union troops, while admitting that the damage was not as extensive as it could have been. In a letter to William A. Graham, he noted:

> I arrived home on Monday, the 20th inst. and found our people in the greatest distress. Sherman's army took all of the horses and mules in their line of march, killed a great many of the cattle and hogs, and destroyed much of the fencing. They robbed almost everyone, both in the town and country, of their corn, forage, and other stores of provisions; and so demoralized our slave population that it will be a long time before masters can again assert and exercise their authority. I think the hope of even a scanty crop in this County, is very faint indeed.
>
> About twenty-five houses in this County (including the Arsenal building and factories) were burned, but I have not heard that the torch was applied to a single private residence which was occupied. . . .
>
> While in Richmond I was told that the "passage of the enemy thro' the country was like the flight of an arrow thro' the air," that "overrunning was not subjugation," etc. Well, this may be true in some sections of the country, but it is far different here. Our people are subjugated—they are crushed in spirit—they have not the heart to do anything but meet together and recount their losses and sufferings.

I have not heard of the killing, by the enemy, of but two of our citizens, & they probably, by impudence, provoked their own death. Neither have I heard of a single case of violence offered to females.[66]

Capt. George W. Pepper offered a slightly different viewpoint of the looters and destroyers. His account also called them "bummers" but defined them as "hangers-on of the army," suggesting that they were not subject to the orders and control of the officers. He penned a negative description that invoked some sarcasm to make his points:

Fancy a ragged man, blackened by the smoke of many a pine knot fire, mounted on a scrawny mule, without a saddle, with a gun, a knapsack, a butcher knife and a plug hat, stealing his way through the pine forests far out on the flanks of a column. Keen on the scent of rebels, or bacon, or silver spoons, or corn or anything valuable, and you have him in mind. Think how you would admire him if you were a lone woman, with a family of small children, far from help, when he blandly inquired where you kept your valuables. Think how you would smile when he pryed open your chests with his bayonet or knocked to pieces your tables, pianos and chairs; tore your bed clothing in three inch strips, and scattered the strips about the yard. The "bummers" say it takes too much time to use keys. Color is no protection from these rough riders. They go through a negro cabin in search of diamonds and gold watches with just as much freedom and vivacity as they "loot" the dwelling of a wealthy planter. They appear to be possessed of a spirit of "pure cussedness." . . . There are hundreds of these mounted men with the column, and they go everywhere. Some of them are loaded down with silverware, gold coin and other valuables. I hazard nothing in saying that three-fifths (in value) of the personal property of the country we passed through was taken.[67]

Because the foragers had often acted out of control, Sherman decided to change and restrict the foraging system. He ordered all foragers dismounted and placed in the ranks. Horses and mules were turned over to the quartermaster corps.[68] That change in policy effectively ended the procedure in Goldsboro, but troops stationed in the countryside felt less inhibited by the order.

Supplies from the quartermaster, however, did not include sufficient food for the horses and mules, especially the large numbers confiscated during the march; that food had always been supplied by foraging. F. L. Castex Sr., a lifelong resident of Goldsboro who was thirteen at the time, described the resulting scenes:

They [Union soldiers] had nothing to feed their horses and mules; so they strayed all over the country dying from starvation. There were dead horses lying all over the town, the streets were full of them. They would throw a little dirt over them but not enough to keep down the odor. They had to do something so they issued orders for the cavalry squadrons to round up all stray horses and mules, drive them down to the Neuse River at old Waynesborough, force them into the river while a regiment of soldiers shot them from the banks. They almost dammed up the river. A great many got by and went into the low grounds of the river. These horses were taken up by the farmers on the south side of the river after the war.[69]

Union general Hawley commented on the situation in southeastern North Carolina, where many citizens attempted to protect themselves from guerrilla bands and Confederate deserters. He advised his field officers to abstain from interference unless the residents proclaimed allegiance to the Union, and then to give assistance only when they could spare troops from more critical duties. He offered a token incentive to any deserters who would enter the Federal lines: they would be paid for their weapons and equipment, but they would not be allowed to leave again.[70]

March 25 (Saturday)

Sherman boarded the train for City Point, Virginia, to confer with General Grant and President Lincoln. Schofield was left in control of the troops at Goldsboro.[71] Word was spreading around Goldsboro that the Ninth New Jersey was to be relieved from provost duty. Citizens signed a petition to retain the unit and presented it to the commanding general.[72] False rumors spread among the citizenry of North Carolina. Catherine Edmondston noted: "We hear that Sherman has lost heavily. We have had three engagements with him, in all of which we have been successful. He is reportedly falling back to Fayetteville." Concerning the situation in that town, she remarked: "We hear sad accounts of the suffering in Fayetteville. Sherman's robbers stripped the town of everything in the way of food & the inhabitants are literally living on *parched corn*. God help them."[73]

March 26 (Sunday)

A diarist from the Ninth New Jersey noted that "three or four of Sherman's 'bummers,' while stealing from neighboring plantations, were shot and killed today. After this the foragers acted with wariness."[74]

General Kilpatrick arrived in Mount Olive. He set up headquarters in the Lemuel W. Kornegay house, reputedly the most handsome structure in the village. His traveling unit, the Third Kentucky Cavalry Regiment, took up camp across the Everettsville-Goldsboro Road on the farm of Bennett Millard Jr.[75] The hospital corps pitched a tent in which to treat some of the wounded and placed others in "The Elms," a house built by Dr. Gideon Roberts about 1860. The village was "completely swamped by soldiers and every night the camp fires so lighted the sky that some residents said it looked like full moonlight."[76] Kilpatrick earned the resentment of local residents by ordering his hostess, Mrs. Kornegay, to taste every dish served to him to see if poison had been added.[77]

March 27 (Monday)

"Bummers" were still active on the outskirts of Goldsboro. Elizabeth Collier noted another incident at her home in Everettsville:

A party of the most desperate fellows burst the back door down and forced their entrance. . . . And now they commenced their sacking of the house and did not cease until they had taken everything to eat the house contained—not leaving us a single mouthful. Curses and oaths were uttered on all sides—it was truly fearful. One fellow remarked in his insolent way, as he was destroying a jar of Brandy Peaches that he really did feel sorry for these people—they had so little. They then told us they intended burning the house that night—made the most desperate threats—they did put fire in three places but the guard extinguished it before it did any injury. Poor Miss Sally had her trunks searched, and her things stolen—while they cursed her every moment calling her *Damned old rebel &c.*[78]

Around Pikeville the Union foragers did a great deal of damage to the property of Sarah Peel Pike, widow of Nathan Pike, for whom the community was named, and also burned the tavern and inn located at the crossroads.[79]

Maj. Gen. Darius N. Couch, commanding the First and Second Divisions of the Twenty-Third Corps, reported to General Schofield from Mosely Hall: "Captain [John W.] Horn, Twelfth New York Cavalry . . . brought in thirteen Federal stragglers whom he found within seven miles of Greenville, plundering houses and tearing the rings from women's fingers."[80]

Special Order No. 66 from Gen. Alfred H. Terry encouraged further destruction by the "bummers" and stragglers. It read: "Col. M. Kerwin, Thirteenth Pennsylvania Cavalry, will, with two battalions of his regiment, proceed to the Black and South Rivers and destroy all the bridges over them south of Clinton. He will also destroy all the flats and ferryboats to be found on those rivers, and as far as possible obstruct the roads leading to the crossings."[81]

According to the *Weekly Conservative* of Raleigh, the men of Johnston's and Wheeler's commands behaved little better than Sherman's "bummers." Governor Vance had received numerous complaints of "illegal and wholesale robberies." The governor attempted to stop the Confederate activities by calling out the Home Guard, but he was unable to assemble a sufficient force.[82] Kemp P. Battle, a lawyer and later president of the University of North Carolina, confirmed the negative view of Wheeler's cavalry. Concerning the unit's passage through Raleigh, he wrote: "The only time I ever carried a weapon with the expectation of possibly being called upon to use it was to defend my horses against robbery by one of our own soldiers. General Wheeler may have been maligned but the lawless conduct of some of his soldiers was generally credited."[83]

With both armies living off the land, conflicts between foraging parties were inevitable. Charles E. Belknap, a Union volunteer, recalled one such encounter: "Out upon the flanks one day a party of Wheeler's men were found; they too were foraging—had their animals well loaded with all sorts of plunder, useful and ornamental. We rushed them, to use a modern term, capturing the outfit, taking a rich prize to camp that night."[84]

Even the horrors of war sometimes have comic interludes. Belknap continued in his memoirs:

The "bummers" had captured a plantation rich in chickens and other useful articles. While the men were busy twisting the necks off the chickens and gathering eggs, a troop of Wheeler's men came down on us like a whirlwind, and drove the boys to the shelter of the woods nearby. When Wheeler's men appeared the lady of the house came out and offered her help to whip the Yankees. "If you want to help us, get up there on that fence and holler at them and dare them to come out for a fair fight." She got upon the top rail and shaking her fist, shouted, "Oh you miserable Yankees. You have taken every chicken on the place." "What's that!" said the Confederate, "taken all the chickens? Then there's nothing left worth fighting for." And he called his men out of the fence corners and rode away, leaving the woman on top of the fence, so busy calling names and shaking fists she did not notice his absence until the "miserable Yankees" returned to gather up odds and ends so hurriedly left.[85]

March 28 (Tuesday)

Gen. Darius N. Couch reported to Schofield that between Kinston and Goldsboro, "women are ravished and robbed by stragglers all over the country."[86] Leaders attempted to maintain discipline among the troops. One soldier was court-martialed and executed for murdering an old man. Another, who had been tried and ordered to be hanged on March 18 for raping a fifty-eight-year-old Wayne County woman, had his death sentence changed to execution by firing squad.[87]

Foraging continued in true "bummer" fashion, despite Sherman's directive. Brig. Gen. John M. Oliver was disturbed by incidents involving members of the Fifteenth Corps: "[T]hey are stripping the people of everything that can sustain life. I saw families of women, children and Negroes who had absolutely nothing to eat, and their houses and quarters stripped of everything—cooking utensils, bedding, crockery, etc. Some rascals are beginning to set fire to the deserted houses of those who have fled to Goldsborough."[88]

Georgia Hicks, a student at St. Mary's School in Raleigh, recorded the activity of Federals at and near the home of her father, Dr. James H. Hicks, who lived near Faison:

In March, the armies of Generals Alfred Howe Terry and Sherman came to Duplin county on their way to Raleigh. . . . I have heard mother say that General Terry, whose headquarters were at the home of my sister, Mrs. C. D. Hill, was always kind and a thorough gentleman, as were the members of his staff, very different from Sherman and his officers. The behavior of Sherman's army around Faison is but a a repetition of the treatment of the people wherever they went.

In the home of Mrs. Rachel Pearsal, her aunt, aged and ill, was thrown from her bed on the floor, so they could look for valuables they thought hidden there.

My courageous mother saw her husband, Doctor James H. Hicks, carried away in the night by the soldiers on the pretext of attending a sick man. . . . He was carried far away and when he was brought back later, he had the appearance of a man that had almost seen death. The ruffians hung him by the neck twice, in their endeavor to secure information as to hidden valuables. They finally released their victim who refused to divulge his secrets. He never recovered from this terrible shock. . . .

One day a man came downstairs with his arms full of silk dresses. Miss Rachel McIver, "sister cousin" of Mrs. Hicks ordered him to put them down. He laughed loud, jumped on his horse and galloped away.[89]

March 30 (Thursday)

Sherman returned to Goldsboro from City Point.[90] Johnson Hagood, brigadier general, CSA, identified 828 men under his command in John F. Hoke's Brigade as absent without leave.[91] The Raleigh *Daily Progress* reported a shooting incident involving a Confederate cavalryman:

We learn that a Cavalryman claiming to belong to Wheeler's command was shot on last Tuesday night [March 28] by Mr. Augustin Morris, a citizen of [Wake] county residing about seven miles west of Raleigh. The Cavalryman went to Mr. Morris' house and ordered some cooking done. Mr. Morris replied that his wife was sick and told the soldier he could go into the kitchen and do his cooking. At this the soldier became "riled" and drew his pistol and fired at Mr. Morris as he entered his house. Mr. Morris seized his shot gun and returned the fire, putting one shot into the back of the soldier's head and another one through one of his ears. The soldier was not dangerously wounded, but has been arrested and taken to headquarters.[92]

William B. Stanton, a member of Hiram B. Granbury's Brigade of a Texas regiment, CSA, wrote to his cousin, Mary Moody: "Granbury's Brig[ade] is counted the best brig in the army to fight and a set of thieves other wise. Our brig behaved shamefully all the way from Tupelo Miss to Raleigh, N.C. The boys had not been paid off for ten months they would not issue Tobacco and that made the boys angry they would break open stores, get the Tobacco and Lichors."[93]

March 31 (Friday)

The execution order of March 28 was carried out. Pvt. James Preble of the Twelfth New York Cavalry was executed for the rape of Letitia Craft near Whitehall (now Seven Springs), about thirteen miles southeast of Goldsboro. The court-martial took place in Kinston, but the death sentence was carried out in Goldsboro. A detailed description of the execution appeared in the *New York Tribune*:

The division arrived on the ground at precisely one o'clock, and was formed in two ranks on three sides of a square, the rear ranks ten paces in rare [rear] of the front rank, which came to an about face when the unfortunate condemned one was paraded through the ranks.

At about twenty minutes to three o'clock, the procession which attended the unfortunate man who was soon to be summarily summoned into the presence of his Maker, made its appearance in the following order: A detachment of the One Hundred and Thirty second New York and Seventeenth Massachusetts Volunteers, under command of Captain Keenan, Acting Provost Marshall, four men carrying a coffin, an ambulance containing the condemned man and his two spiritual advisors, the Reverend H. M. Bacon, Chaplain of the Twenty-fifth Massachusetts. Upon arriving on the ground, the unfortunate man was taken from the ambulance and escorted in mournful procession with the Drum Corps playing the dead march through the ranks forming three sides of the square.

James Preble did not appear to be more than twenty years of age, and about six feet in height; his appearance in no way gave indication of the brutality which would naturally be supposed to characterize the appearance of one proved to have been guilty of so heinous an offense. He marched with a remarkably steady step all the way around the square, and but seldom raised his eyes from the ground.

In the center of the space in the open side of the square, Preble's grave was dug and on arriving at it, after marching around the square, the procession halted, and the proceedings and sentence of the court-martial, together with the order for execution, was read by the

Provost Marshall, after which he knelt down by his coffin, with the Chaplain in attendance, and prayed for about five minutes, when his eyes were bandaged with a white handkerchief, and the firing party, consisting of twelve men from the One Hundred and Thirty-second New York and Seventeenth Pennsylvania were formed in line about twelve paces in front of him.

At precisely five minutes past three the order to "make ready, aim, and fire" was delivered in a clear and audible tone by the Acting Provost Marshall, and the unfortunate man fell down dead pierced with four balls, one through the neck and three through the breast. He was immediately examined by the Provost Marshall and the surgeon in attendance and pronounced dead.

The whole division was then marched past the corpse which was placed on top of the coffin, by the columns of companies, and filed back to their quarters. This will doubtless prove, as it is intended it should, a warning to evil disposed and reckless men, and they will know acts of barbarity will not be tolerated in an army whose purpose is to restore law and order.[94]

F. L. Castex, a witness to the execution, later recalled the event. His account was essentially the same as the newspaper's, except that he recalled twenty-four men in the firing squad, twelve of whom had blanks in their weapons. He also added that the spectacle took place "where the city waterworks are now located" [in 1934] and that a piece of white paper was pinned on Preble's left breast to serve as a target.[95]

The court-martial and execution were carried out under orders from General Schofield. Castex offered a clear delineation between Generals Schofield and Sherman: "General Schofield had his men under complete military control, no stragglers or burners. The only depredation I saw or heard of was that they destroyed fences and outhouses to make fires to cook with. General Sherman permitted all kinds of depredations and allowed an army of stragglers, thieves, and burners to follow in his wake which carried out the boast that 'A crow would starve to death flying over his trail.' "[96]

Fear of Sherman's potential movements gripped the countryside, as illustrated by Catherine Edmondston's entry in her diary on March 31:

Johnston's lines reach from Louisburg to Tarboro. The line of the Tar [River] is to be defended, so we are now told. Should he [Johnston] continue to fall back, the Roanoke is the next defensible point. We should then be in the storm of War & suffer as our Southern compatriots have done. In Fayetteville the actual pangs of hunger have been felt by the whole population. For days they have subsisted on parched corn & a little rice. From their fate Good Lord Deliver us![97]

Even Sherman's own men were uncertain of his ultimate destination, though most assumed it would be Richmond. An Iowa sergeant commented: "It is the talk with the Boys now that our next move will be in the direction of Richmond, but they say it is hard to tell which way Crazy Bill will go for he goes where ever he wants to and the rebs cant [sic] help themselves."[98]

April 1 (Saturday)

Brig. Gen. Joseph R. Hawley reported to Schofield: "The authority of the Government is weakened by the impunity with which stragglers, deserters from either army, marauders, bummers, and strolling vagabonds, negroes, and whites commit outrages upon the inhabitants. To say nothing of insults and plundering, there have been three cases of rape and one of murder."[99]

April 2 (Sunday)

Catherine Edmondston commented on the poor and unreliable state of communications:"Our news depends on the disposition of the person from whom we get it. Bro[ther] writes that Sherman can go anywhere, for Johnston is too weak to oppose him, 'whilst Maj. Gale [Seaton E. Gales, former adjutant of the Fourteenth North Carolina Regiment] assures us that the army is in fine spirits & wants for nothing."[100]

April 3 (Monday)

Officers under the command of General Wheeler issued a testimonial in behalf of their leader and denied committing the outrages attributed to the Confederate cavalry. In the face of numerous accusations against Wheeler's unit, Col. E. E. Portlock Jr., on general inspection from the War Department, conducted an independent investigation of the cavalry's conduct in Georgia and the Carolinas. The following are excerpts from the longer version of Portlock's report:

Through all the regions of the country in which these depredations are said to have been committed, orders were enforced from Generals Beauregard, Bragg, Hardee and from the War Department, requiring the destruction of subsistence, mills, etc., and the removal of stock which could be useful to the enemy, from his line of march. During most of this time General Wheeler's corps was alone, and the execution of this unpleasant duty devolved entirely upon it. Probably during the entire existence of this war no other command has been called upon to execute such unpalatable orders.

My own experience while with this corps showed me that citizens would procrastinate in the removal of stock until it became necessary to take forcible possession of it to prevent the enemy from getting it. As before remarked, the natural disposition of all men is to complain at losses, and I have frequently heard remarks made by citizens of this character, "Possibly I can beg the Federals to let me keep my corn and stock"; "If the Federals take my property I cannot help it, but I do not nor cannot tolerate its being forcibly taken by our own soldiers." Forgetful of the fact that they had to deal with a ruthless foe, whose path was lit with the flames of burning houses, whose wagons and knapsacks were loaded with plunder, even jewels robbed from defenceless females; whose boast was the misery, ruin and dishonor they had brought on helpless men, women and children—they, these citizens, clung with deathlike tenacity to that which would benefit our enemy and aid him in the work of subjugation; preferring to trust in his tender mercies that which should have been laid on the altar of patriotism and liberty; for everything necessary to secure our independence (without which property and all other mercenary considerations are but the passing winds) should have been freely given. It was often necessary to take subsistence and stock from plantations which the owner had deserted, and on which there was no one to give a receipt. In other instances the proximity of the enemy rendered it impossible to give receipts, and in still other instances officers were doubtless negligent in giving proper certificates for property thus taken or destroyed, and sometimes exceeded their orders in so doing. . . .

Accompanying this are certificates taken from citizens by these officers and selected by me from a large number. In some of them various charges are made, but nothing positive enough to detect the offender; generally they are favorable to the character and prominence of the corps. Some spoke of the killing of hogs and chickens, and a few of horses stolen. These are fair specimens, and are signed by the various farmers in each vicinity or settlement. General Wheeler's letter and Colonel [I. W.] Avery's report both go to show that there were a class of people who followed in the wake of the army, perpetrating outrages in the name of this corps, and that even Sherman clothed some of his men in Confederate uniform, who passed themselves off as Wheeler's cavalry, with the double purpose of obtaining information and to bring the cavalry into disrepute by plundering [under] its name. . . .

No one who visits this corps and observes closely can fail to be impressed with the idea that these men cannot be the desperadoes they are often said to be. Many of them prior to the war were possessed of means; nearly all are volunteers and the numbers which designate the regiments show that they were among the first to enter the service. . . . Men who thus follow the path of duty unflinchingly cannot be lost to all sense of honor and respect, and must be actuated by high and lofty principles. That there are bad men in this corps as in all others is admitted, but it is my deliberate conviction that were all the crimes charged to this corps perpetrated by the bad men in it, it would be necessary to double the length of days to enable them to acomplish the task, operating in a country filled with deserters and released penitentiary convicts, who have followed them as the vulture does a corpse, plundering in their name. The good men of the corps feel deeply the obloquy cast upon them, as it paralyzes their arms in time of danger. . . . Here and there patient re-search [sic] will reveal the fact that some officer exceeded his orders and overstepped his authority, or that some man committed an act of outrage, but the general opinion as it is now fast maturing, will do justice to General Wheeler's corps.[101]

April 4 (Tuesday)

Residents of the Roanoke valley were still fearful of Union troops in the vicinity: "News tonight of a raid through Northampton County towards Weldon. We hear that Jackson a small town about 12 miles from us was burned in the night without giving the inhabitants a warning or allowing them to save anything. This is negro news but is considered reliable. What fiends in human shape are our enemies." The burning of Jackson proved to be a false rumor, however.[102]

Local farmers, whose livestock had been appropriated, appealed to Sherman for some horses to till the fields for planting new crops. The general replied: "I cannot undertake to supply horses or to encourage peaceful industry in North Carolina until the State shall perform some public act showing that, as to her, the war is over. I sympathize with the distress of families, but cannot undertake to extend relief to individuals."[103]

April 5 (Wednesday)

Sherman issued Special Field Order No. 48. The objective was to move his army north of the Roanoke River and to place himself in a position to assist General Grant in the Richmond campaign.[104]

E. J. Cleveland of the Ninth New Jersey Volunteers reported on efforts to obtain spending money: "Peddling on the streets is forbidden but on almost every corner were boys of Sherman's army selling tobacco, watches, silver, etc. captured in the late march. Many of the citizens sell little notions from their front porches."[105] One of those "entrepreneurs of necessity" was F. L. Castex, identified above. He recalled the episode:

I remember very well when the General [Schofield] told my Mother that he wanted the front part of our house and sent his soldiers in and moved us into the dining room. Now Mother and I were not alone. He proved to be a gentleman and did us several favors.

When a big four-horse army wagon drove into our yard loaded with supplies for the General, he gave my Mother a lot of groceries and she made cakes and I peddled them. I got money enough ahead to go to New Bern. In about four days after the army got in here, they had the trains coming in from New Bern bringing in supplies, etc. I asked the General if he would get me a pass to New Bern and return one, which he did. I went down in a box car, bought me some oranges, lemons, tobacco, cigars, candy and had them put on a flat car. The train got into Goldsboro before day and I sat on those boxes all night. Next morning I got some help to take them home.

I took three or four planks off our smokehouse and made me a stand on the corner where the George Crabtree house is now [1934] and started in business for myself selling lemonade, cakes and the like. We had a guard both night and day in front of our house, and they had instructions not to let anyone molest my stand. I moved my stock in the house at night.[106]

General Johnston received dispatches stating that the Confederate administration had evacuated Richmond on April 2.[107] News of Richmond's fall threw the South into a state of gloom and despair. Catherine Edmondston offered a description of conditions in eastern North Carolina:

I sit stunned & am unable to look forward to a single day, to a single consequence in the future. I do not even feel the enormities practised by the enemy on our neighbors in Northampton! The fact that they were reported as being in retreat last night failed to animate me. [Mr.] Jacob's house was not burned [as reported the previous day], but his neighbor [Littleton] Norwood's cotton was. . . . Mr. [M. W.] Smallwood was robbed of everything and had several shots fired at him but succeeded in making his escape. Dr. [C. G. C.] Moore's horses every one taken. In short the country swept of horses and provisions and utterly sacked.[108]

April 6 (Thursday)

Sherman received official word of Richmond's fall. Grant telegraphed Sherman that "the rebel armies are now the only strategic points." Sherman altered Special Order No. 48 to make objectives the capture of Raleigh and the capitulation of Johnston's remaining army.[109]

E. J. Cleveland commented on problems within the ranks of the Union troops:

Last night disorderly soldiers in the streets kept the patrols trotting all the time. Houses containing certain classes of women were surrounded by large gangs which had to be continually dispersed. These fellows of the 15th and 17th Corps entertain a perfect hatred of the 9th N.J. During the night several shots were fired but no one could be found who was responsible. Three poor women were given shelter in the guard house. The "prison room" was well filled with civilians, negroes, rebel deserters and soldiers.[110]

April 6–9 (Thursday–Sunday)

Rumors of the fall of Richmond circulated through the Confederate camp. Morale plummeted, and desertions increased by leaps and bounds. Gen. Lafayette McLaws had to keep two patrols out each day just to arrest men attempting to desert the ranks.[111] On April 9 Johnston ordered the burning of the bridges over the Roanoke at Gaston and Weldon and the impressment of all the food and supplies "for man or beast" lying between Goldsboro and those bridges—much to the anguish and protests of the local residents. Later that day he received intelligence that Sherman was planning to move on Raleigh the following morning.[112]

April 10 (Monday)

Sherman issued marching orders. Slocum's left wing, supported by the Twenty-Third Corps, took two direct roads for Smithfield. The right wing was to make a circuit to the right by Pikeville and Whitley's Mill, with one division swinging around by Nahunta and Beulah. Terry's and Kilpatrick's troops were ordered to move in the same general direction by way of Cox's Bridge.[113]

Johnston sent orders to impress all livestock, goods, and matériel throughout the countryside that could be used by Union troops. Local residents were disillusioned with the Confederate government and the actions of retreating troops. Catherine Edmondston expressed the concern:

Yesterday [April 10] came the Impressing officers with orders from Gen Johnston to *take all the best of our team*, to leave us only the worthless & the inferior. The order runs, "take all that will be of service to the enemy." The feeling against it is intense throughout the country. We think that as the Government confessedly is too weak to protect us, that at least it ought not thus to deprive us of the means of making a support—say to us, *"take care of yourselves"* & let us do the best we can; but no, this morning the best two mules we have here were taken & as I write I see six of the pick of the team at Looking Glass [another family plantation] & Mr. E's [Edmondston's] new blooded Filly, for which he gave $5000 not two months since, coming up—a sad procession to join those already impressed. Our premises are used as a temporary depot for them & there are now 50 mules & horses, the very best in the whole country, wandering up and down there, coupled by twos together, in a most disconsolate forlorn & homesick manner. I would think less of it were I not sure it is impossible in the Government to feed them for one month. In a few weeks their bones will whiten the red clay hills of Warren & Granville through which Johnston returns and we shall not have even the poor satisfaction of knowing that they aided the cause for that short period.

Upon the heels of the horse impressors is to come another gang with direction to take all our meat save three months supply! The Yankees themselves could hardly do worse. We have given & freely given all we could spare & were we asked to give more and live on vegetables, would do it cheerfully & willingly for the sake of *the Cause*, but this forced patriotism is not the thing, is not the way to treat a free & generous people, & ere long hearts will be alienated away from the Government & system that thus tramples on our rights, our feelings, & our sacred honor.[114]

A growing despair made its way from the people to the governor's office. One woman, in the best literary style she could muster, sent a plea to Vance:

For the sake of suffering women and children, do try and stop this cruel war. here I am without one mouthful to eat for myself and five children and God only knows when I will get something now you know as well as you have a head that it is impossible to whip they Yankees, therefore I beg you for God sake to try and make peace on some terms, and let they rest of they poor men come home and try to make something to eat, my husband has been killed, and if they all stay till they are dead, what in the name of God will become of us poor women and children?[115]

Johnston located his army in and around Smithfield. He placed cavalry units in observation of Sherman's army, with Wheeler to the north and Butler to the west. A skirmish between the cavalry units and the First Division of the Twentieth Corps ensued about a mile east of Moccasin Swamp on the northerly road to Smithfield. Another took place near Nahunta. The Confederate cavalries were pushed back in fighting near Beulah and Pikeville. Johnston then pulled his troops back to Raleigh.[116]

April 11 (Tuesday)

At 1:00 A.M. Johnston (then at Raleigh) received a telegram from Jefferson Davis stating that Lee had surrendered on April 9.[117] About noon, the Third Division of the Fourteenth Corps became the first of Sherman's army to enter Smithfield. Confederates offered some resistance by firing from barricades thrown up in the town but were forced to retreat by afternoon. They burned the bridge across the Neuse River on the west side of town as they retreated toward Raleigh. The Twentieth Corps reached Smithfield at 2:00 P.M. The Union troops burned only the stocks at the old jail in Smithfield. They did rifle and dump the archival materials in the courthouse, causing damage to and some loss of the Johnston County records.[118]

The Seventeenth Corps moved into camp at Pine Level. General Howard sent a dispatch to Sherman asking if the policy of destruction of mills and factories was still in effect. Sherman replied that the Lowell Factory was not to be destroyed at that time. He then added: "I will wait our reception at Raleigh to shape our general policy. You will instruct General Logan to exact bonds that the factory shall not be used for the Confederacy. Of course, the bond is not worth a cent, but if the factory owners do not abide by the conditions, they cannot expect any mercy the next time."[119]

Gen. Jacob D. Cox recorded in his journal: "The stragglers in the army have become much worse than they were in the Atlanta campaign. Two of the best residences along our road were burned today. One, the house of a Mr. Atkinson where I stopped at noon to take lunch, was in flames half an hour after we left it; the soldiers suspect him of being a conscription agent for the rebel government, and this may account for his house being burned."[120]

At 4:30 P.M. President Davis directed Johnston to leave his troops in Raleigh under the command of General Hardee and report to him in Greensboro.[121] During the night, the Union troops received word of Lee's surrender. Great jubilation and celebrations continued throughout the night and early morning.[122]

Sherman's march from Goldsboro to Smithfield occasioned fear and anguish among the local residents. Anna L. Fuller, a resident of Franklin County, though not in the direct line of march, nevertheless shared the concerns of her fellow countrymen. She confided to her diary:

> [It is a] dreadful state of suspense we are in about the Yankees coming among us . . . we shall soon be if we are not already in the Yankee lines and I am sure I never looked to anything with more fearful apprehension, than I do to their coming among us. We have been planning all day how to secreet [sic] our valuables. Tonight Sister Mary and myself have carried several [illegible] of things to what we consider a place of safety. I fear some evil eye was upon us, to betray us, but hope not.[123]

NOTES

1. *The War of the Rebellion: A Compilation of the Official Records of the Union and Confederate Armies*, ser. 1, 47, pt. 2:794, 800 (hereafter cited as *Official Records . . . Armies*); John G. Barrett, *Sherman's March through the Carolinas* (Chapel Hill: University of North Carolina Press, 1956), 147–148; Samuel Toombs, *Reminiscences of the War, Comprising a Detailed Account of the Experiences of the Thirteenth Regiment New Jersey Volunteers* (Orange, N.J.: Printed at the Journal office, 1878), 209.

2. Barrett, *Sherman's March*, 148–149.

3. *Official Records . . . Armies*, ser. 1, 47, pt. 2:834–835, 1375, 1392.

4. *Official Records . . . Armies*, ser. 1, 47, pt. 1:1084; Barrett, *Sherman's March*, 150; Jessie S. Smith, "On the Battle Field at Averasboro, N.C.," *Confederate Veteran* 34 (February 1926): 48–49.

5. *Official Records . . . Armies*, ser. 1, 47, pt. 1:880, 1084; William Tecumseh Sherman, *Memoirs of General W. T. Sherman* (New York: Library of America, 1990 [reprint of 1886 edition]), 782; Toombs, *Reminiscences of the War*, 209.

6. Sherman, *Memoirs*, 782–783; *Official Records . . . Armies*, ser. 1, 47, pt. 1:1084.

7. *Official Records . . . Armies*, ser. 1, 47, pt. 1:1084–1085; Barrett, *Sherman's March*, 152–154; Toombs, *Reminscences of the War*, 209–210; Smith, "Battle Field at Averasboro," 48.

8. Edwin E. Bryant, *History of the Third Regiment of Wisconsin Veteran Volunteer Infantry, 1861–1865* (Madison: Veteran Association of the Regiment, 1891), 317; E. B. Long, *The Civil War Day by Day: An Almanac, 1861–1865* (Garden City, N.J.: Doubleday and Co., 1971), 653.

9. Katharine M. Jones, *When Sherman Came: Southern Women and the "Great March"* (Indianapolis: Bobbs-Merrill, 1964), 289; Smith, "Battle Field at Averasboro," 48–49.

10. Jones, *When Sherman Came*, 290; Smith, "Battle Field at Averasboro," 48–49.

11. The letter from Janie Smith to her friend Janie Roberson was written April 12, 1865, and preserved by the family over the years. It appeared in an article in the *Raleigh News and Observer* on May 10, 1953.

12. Smith, "Battle Field at Averasboro," 49.

13. Sherman, *Memoirs*, 784; Bryant, *Third Regiment of Wisconsin*, 317; Jones, *When Sherman Came*, 289–290.

14. Sherman, *Memoirs*, 784; *Official Records . . . Armies*, ser. 1, 47, pt. 1:1084; John F. Marszalek, *Sherman: A Soldier's Passion for Order* (New York: Free Press, 1993), 330. Marszalek contends that "Sherman angrily sent word that in retaliation for this outrage [the treatment of Captain Duncan], Alfred Rhett should be taken from his horse and forced to walk to prison." His cited evidence fails, however, to support his claim of such a statement, and none could be found in the orders issued for days after the engagement.

15. The letter was written on March 16, 1865. J. G. de Roulhac Hamilton, ed., *The Correspondence of Jonathan Worth*, 2 vols. (Raleigh: North Carolina Historical Commission, 1909), 1:368–369.

16. Hamilton, *Correspondence of Jonathan Worth*, 1:369–370.

17. *Official Records . . . Armies*, ser. 1, 47, pt. 2:1411, 1416.

18. Sherman, *Memoirs*, 784; Bryant, *Third Regiment of Wisconsin*, 317; Jones, *When Sherman Came*, 289–290.

19. *Official Records . . . Armies*, ser. 1, 47, pt. 2:1425.

20. Barrett, *Sherman's March*, 158.

21. Joseph E. Johnston, *Narrative of Military Operations Directed, During the Late War Between the States* (Bloomington: Indiana University Press, 1959), 384.

22. *Official Records . . . Armies*, ser. 1, 47, pt. 2:885–886; Sherman, *Memoirs*, 785.

23. Barrett, *Sherman's March*, 161.

24. Barrett, *Sherman's March*, 161–162; Sherman, *Memoirs*, 785; *Official Records . . . Armies*, ser. 1, 47, pt. 2:886.

25. Johnston, *Narrative*, 385; Long, *The Civil War Day by Day*, 654.

26. Barrett, *Sherman's March*, 163–164; Sherman, *Memoirs*, 785; Toombs, *Reminiscences of the War*, 214; *Official Records . . . Armies*, ser. 1, 47, pt. 1:25, pt. 2:908–909.

27. Allan S. Gleason, ed., "The Military Services and Record of Sgt. Charles H. Dickinson, 1862–1865" (copy of unpublished manuscript), 48. Dickinson was a member of the Twenty-second Wisconsin Volunteers and kept a diary of his service.

28. *Official Records . . . Armies*, ser. 1, 47, pt. 1:121, 253; Johnston, *Narrative*, 390; Toombs, *Reminiscences of the War*, 216; Long, *The Civil War Day by Day*, 655.

29. Recorded in Jones, *When Sherman Came*, 290.

30. *Raleigh Daily Progress*, March 20, 1865.

31. *Official Records . . . Armies*, ser. 1, 47, pt. 2:927.

32. Johnston, *Narrative*, 390–393; Sherman, *Memoirs*, 787–788; Long, *The Civil War Day by Day*, 655.

33. George Ward Nichols, *The Story of the Great March* (New York: Harper and Brothers, 1865; Williamston, Mass.: Corner House Publishers, 1972), 266.

34. Bryant, *Third Regiment of Wisconsin*, 326.

35. *Official Records . . . Armies*, ser. 1, 47, pt. 2:942; excerpt from diary of a Union soldier named Drake, quoted in Bob Johnson and Charles S. Norwood, eds., *History of Wayne County: A Collection of Historical Stories* (Goldsboro: Wayne County Historical Association, 1979), 157.

36. *Official Records . . . Armies*, ser. 1, 47, pt. 2:1453; Barrett, *Sherman's March*, 185.

37. Johnson and Norwood, *Wayne County*, 151, 154.

38. Johnson and Norwood, *Wayne County*, 157–158, quoting Drake diary.

39. Nichols, *Story of the Great March*, 278.

40. Nichols, *Story of the Great March*, 278.

41. Beth G. Crabtree and James W. Patton, eds., *"Journal of a Secesh Lady": The Diary of Catherine Ann Devereux Edmondston, 1860–1866* (Raleigh: Division of Archives and History, 1979), 682 (hereafter cited as Crabtree and Patton, *Edmondston Diary*).

42. Sherman, *Memoirs*, 788; *Official Records . . . Armies*, ser. 1, 47, pt. 1:28.

43. *Official Records . . . Armies*, ser. 1, 47, pt. 2:959–960.

44. *Official Records . . . Armies*, ser. 1, 47, pt. 3:14. See Union general Joseph R. Hawley, commander of Wilmington District, to B. M. Richardson, March 24, 1865. See also John G. Barrett, *The Civil War in North Carolina* (Chapel Hill: University of North Carolina Press, 1963), 341.

45. *Official Records . . . Armies*, ser. 1, 47, pt. 2:1451.

46. Johnson and Norwood, *Wayne County*, 158.

47. *Official Records . . . Armies*, ser. 1, 47, pt. 2, 1453.

48. Recollections of F. L. Castex Jr., then a young man of thirteen; Johnson and Norwood, *Wayne County*, 163.

49. Barrett, *Sherman's March*, 185; Sherman, *Memoirs*, 788; Long, *The Civil War Day by Day*, 656; *Heritage of Wayne County, 1982* (Goldsboro: Wayne County Historical Association, 1982), 19.

50. Johnson and Norwood, *Wayne County*, 151–152.

51. Quoted in Barrett, *Sherman's March*, 186–187.

52. Quoted in Johnson and Norwood, *Wayne County*, 155.

53. Bryant, *Third Regiment of Wisconsin*, 327; Johnson and Norwood, *Wayne County*, 155.

54. Quotes taken from Johnson and Norwood, *Wayne County*, 155.

55. Quoted in Johnson and Norwood, *Wayne County*, 156.

56. J. G. de Roulhac Hamilton et al., eds., *The Papers of William Alexander Graham*, 8 vols. (Raleigh: Department of Archives and History, 1957–1992), 6:286 (hereafter cited as Hamilton et al., *Graham Papers*).

57. Sherman, *Memoirs*, 799. See letter to General Grant, March 24, 1865. See also closing of same letter, p. 800, for reference to housing.

58. *Official Records . . . Armies*, ser. 1, 47, pt. 3:11–12.

59. Diary entry for March 24 quoted in Johnson and Norwood, *Wayne County*, 158.

60. *Winston Western Sentinel*, March 30, 1865.

61. *Sketches of War History, 1861–1865: Papers Read Before the Ohio Commandery of the Military Order of the Loyal Legion of the United States, 1883–1886*, 5 vols. (Cincinnati: Robert Clarke and Co., 1888), 1:13–14.

62. In late March 1865 the commander was Manning F. Force. *Sketches of War History*, 1:11.

63. Charles E. Belknap, "Recollections of a Bummer," in *The War of the 'Sixties*, ed. E. R. Hutchins (New York: Neale Publishing Company, 1912), 345.

64. Nichols, *Story of the Great March*, 276. For a different view, see the description by Eleanor B. Powell in Johnson and Norwood, *Wayne County*, 155.

65. *Official Records . . . Armies,* ser. 1, 47, pt. 3:46.

66. Hamilton et al., *Graham Papers*, 6:287.

67. George W. Pepper, *Personal Recollections of Sherman's Campaigns in Georgia and the Carolinas* (Zanesville, Ohio: Hugh Dunne, 1866), 275–276.

68. *Official Records . . . Armies*, ser. 1, 47, pt. 2:972.

69. Quoted in Johnson and Norwood, *Wayne County*, 164.

70. *Official Records . . . Armies*, ser. 1, 47, pt. 3:14.

71. Sherman, *Memoirs*, 810.

72. Recorded in diary of member of the Ninth New Jersey and quoted in Johnson and Norwood, *Wayne County*, 158.

73. Crabtree and Patton, *Edmondston Diary*, 684–685.

74. Entry quoted in Johnson and Norwood, *Wayne County*, 158.

75. *Heritage of Wayne County*, 19. For the reorganization of the Union cavalry, see Sherman, *Memoirs*, 828.

76. *Heritage of Wayne County*, 19.

77. *Heritage of Wayne County*, 19.

78. Jones, *When Sherman Came*, 290.

79. *Heritage of Wayne County*, 19. See also historical sketch of Pikeville by Bob Johnson in Johnson and Norwood, *Wayne County*, 84. See also *Official Records . . . Armies*, ser. 1, 47, pt. 3:123.

80. Thomas Bland Keys, *The Uncivil War: Union Army and Navy Excesses in the Official Records* (Biloxi, Miss.: Beauvoir Press, 1991), 129.

81. *Official Records . . . Armies*, ser. 1, 47, pt. 3:38.

82. *Raleigh Weekly Conservative*, April 5, 1865. See Richard E. Yates, "Governor Vance and the End of the War in North Carolina," *North Carolina Historical Review* 18 (October 1941): 326.

83. Kemp Plummer Battle, *Memories of an Old-Time Tar Heel*, ed. William James Battle (Chapel Hill: University of North Carolina Press, 1945), 191.

84. Belknap, "Recollections of a Bummer," 347.

85. Belknap, "Recollections of a Bummer," 349.

86. Keys, *The Uncivil War*, 129.

87. Barrett, *Sherman's March*, 193–194; Johnson and Norwood, *Wayne County*, 163–164. The transcript of the court-martial proceedings are filed in Record Group 153: Proceedings of the U.S. Army General Courts-Martial, 1809–1898, National Archives, Washington, D.C., 003428—James Preble. Copy supplied to Research Branch courtesy Mark Bradley, Raleigh.

88. Keys, *The Uncivil War*, 129.

89. Jones, *When Sherman Came*, 296.

90. Sherman, *Memoirs*, 819.

91. Johnson Hagood, *Memoirs of the War of Secession From the Original Manuscripts of Johnson Hagood* (Columbia: The State Company, 1910), 365.

92. *Raleigh Daily Progress*, March 30, 1865.

93. William E. Stanton Letters, 1861–1865, University of Texas Archives, Austin, Texas. A monument to the Texas troops at Bentonville acknowledges the service of Granbury's Brigade. Information from the research of Mark Bradley of Raleigh and used with his permission.

94. Quoted in full in Johnson and Norwood, *Wayne County*, 160-161.

95. Johnson and Norwood, *Wayne County*, 164.

96. Johnson and Norwood, *Wayne County*, 164.

97. Crabtree and Patton, *Edmondston Diary*, 686.

98. Joseph T. Glatthaar, *The March to the Sea and Beyond: Sherman's Troops in the Savannah and Carolinas Campaigns* (New York: New York University Press, 1985), 174.

99. Keys, *The Uncivil War*, 129–130.

100. Crabtree and Patton, *Edmondston Diary*, 687.

101. "Inspection Report Made by Colonel E. E. Portlock, Jr. on General Inspection Duties From War Department, March and April, 1865," in William Carey Dodson and Joseph Wheeler, *Campaigns of Wheeler and His Cavalry, 1862–1865* (Atlanta: Hudgins Publishing Company, 1900), 420–430.

102. Crabtree and Patton, *Edmondston Diary*, 688.

103. Response quoted verbatim in Johnson and Norwood, *Wayne County*, 156–157. See also Marszalek, *Sherman*, 339, quoting the *Cincinnati Commercial*, April 18, 1865.

104. Sherman, *Memoirs*, 829–830.

105. Diary entry quoted in Johnson and Norwood, *Wayne County*, 159.

106. Account published in Johnson and Norwood, *Wayne County*, 164–165.

107. Johnston, *Narrative*, 395.

108. Crabtree and Patton, *Edmondston Diary*, 689.

109. Sherman, *Memoirs*, 831; Barrett, *Sherman's March*, 199.

110. Diary entry quoted in Johnson and Norwood, *Wayne County*, 159.

111. McLaws's Order Book, 1865, p. 35, in Barrett, *Sherman's March*, 201.

112. Jonathan Worth to J. J. Jackson, April 9, 1865, Hamilton, *Correspondence of Jonathan Worth*, 1:379; Johnston, *Narrative*, 396.

113. *Official Records . . . Armies*, ser. 1, 47, pt. 3:123.

114. Crabtree and Patton, *Edmondston Diary*, 691–692.

115. Anonymous letter to Zebulon B. Vance, undated, Governors Papers, Zebulon B. Vance, Governors Papers, State Archives, Division of Archives and History, Raleigh. The letter is also quoted in Yates, "Governor Vance and the End of the War," 319.

116. Johnston, *Narrative*, 396; *Official Records . . . Armies*, ser. 1, 47, pt. 1:249, 603, 614, 626–627.

117. Johnston, *Narrative*, 396.

118. Barrett, *Sherman's March*, 204–205.

119. Barrett, *Sherman's March*, 206; *Official Records . . . Armies*, ser. 1, 47, pt. 3:165.

120. *Official Records . . . Armies*, ser. 1, 47, pt. 1:936. See entry for April 11.

121. Johnston, *Narrative*, 396.

122. Sherman, *Memoirs*, 832; Barrett, *Sherman's March*, 207–208.

123. Diary of Anna L. Fuller, April 11, 1865, Cecil W. Robbins Library, Louisburg College, Louisburg.

PART 3

April 12–May 4, 1865

April 12 (Wednesday)

Around midnight, as April 11 became April 12, Gen. Joseph E. Johnston boarded a train leaving Raleigh bound for Greensboro. There, the following morning, in meetings with Pres. Jefferson Davis and members of his cabinet, the fate of the Confederate States of America rested in the balance. The setting was inauspicious; railroad cars housed the political and military leaders of the rebel government.

General Johnston was initially the guest of Gen. P. G. T. Beauregard, his second-in-command in the Carolinas Campaign. Together they walked from his quarters to those of the Confederate president, who was in the company of his secretary of state, Judah P. Benjamin; secretary of the treasury, John H. Reagan; and secretary of the navy, Stephen R. Mallory. Secretary of War John C. Breckinridge arrived and confirmed the news of the surrender of Gen. Robert E. Lee's army at Appomattox Courthouse. Johnston and Beauregard advised the party that the "only power of government left in the President's hands was that of terminating the war, and that this power should be exercised without more delay." As a consequence, the waning of the war was set in motion.[1]

Eighty miles to the east, in Raleigh, Confederates hurriedly evacuated the capital city in anticipation of the arrival of Gen. William T. Sherman's forces. At midday Capt. W. E. Stoney, officer in a South Carolina brigade, took note of the "immense quantities of stores destroyed and abandoned."[2] Cornelia Phillips Spencer of Chapel Hill, to whom modern-day chroniclers of the final days of the war in North Carolina are indebted for her firsthand account, recorded this scene:

An immense amount of State property had been removed to various points along the Central Railroad. Some forty thousand blankets, overcoats, clothes, and English cloth equal to at least one hundred thousand suits complete; leather and shoes equal to ten thousand pairs; great quantities of cotton cloth and yarns, and cotton-cards; six thousand scythe-blades; one

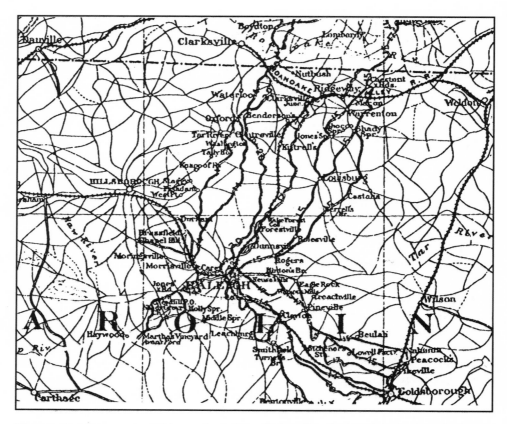

Sherman's men traversed this portion of North Carolina during their final twenty-three days in the state, April 12 to May 4, 1865. Detail of map from *The Official Atlas of the Civil War* (New York and London: Thomas Yoseloff, 1958; reprint of Calvin D. Cowles [comp.], *Atlas to Accompany the Official Records of the Union and Confederate Armies . . .* [Washington: Government Printing Office, 1891–1895]), plate CXVII.

hundred and fifty thousand pounds of bacon; forty thousand bushels of corn; a very large stock of imported medical stores; and many other articles of great value, together with the public records, Treasury and Literary Board, and other effects, were most deposited at Graham, Greensboro, and Salisbury.[3]

State treasurer Jonathan Worth, who later in 1865 served as governor of North Carolina, took charge of efforts to remove state valuables from Raleigh. The last wagonload left the city shortly before 9:00 P.M. Progress was slow; by the following day the departing Confederates had advanced only as far as Durham's Station.[4]

As Johnston's departing army passed through Raleigh on April 12, female students at St. Mary's School carried dinner out to the school gates and gave it to the soldiers. Kate McKimmon, one of the students, later recalled the scene and contrasted the condition of the troops with that of the Union soldiers who followed soon after: "Well do I remember the day, April 12, 1865. Throughout Raleigh, all along their march, food and water were carried to them. The appearance of that brave body of men, emaciated from lack of food, did not tend to produce any enjoyment in seeing the Yankee army, fat, sleek, with banners flying, drums beating, pass through our city, three days being required to accomplish it."[5]

For the people of Raleigh, Wednesday, April 12, was the calm before the storm. They hid personal property of value in yards, under fence posts, and in creek beds. "Every suggestion of ingenuity," according to Cornelia Phillips Spencer, "had been put in practice by the citizens in concealing their private property." Mrs. Spencer reviled the foraging Yankees, the "snappers up of even such unconsidered trifles as an old negro's silver watch or a baby's corals—from the hands of such as these what was to be expected; what nook, or cranny, or foot of inclosed ground would be safe from their search!"[6]

Sherman received the news of Gen. Robert E. Lee's surrender at Appomattox overnight and announced the report to his troops in Special Field Order No. 54: "The General commanding announces to the army that he has official notice from General Grant that General Lee surrendered to him his entire army, on the 9th inst., at Appomattox Court-House, Virginia. Glory to God and our country, and all honor to our comrades in arms, toward whom we are marching! A little more labor, a little more toil on our part, the great race is won, and our Government stands regenerated, after four long years of war."[7] This news, according to Sherman, resulted in a "perfect *furore* of rejoicing." It heralded an imminent end to all hostilities, inasmuch as Johnston, as all knew, had practically no army to oppose Sherman's. The only question, Sherman posed, was whether Johnston would allow his men to disperse into guerrilla bands and thereby maintain a prolonged conflict without foreseeable end. At 5:00 A.M. on April 12 Sherman wired Gen. Ulysses S. Grant, welcoming the news of the surrender and stating that he would seek the same "magnanimous and liberal" terms from Johnston.[8]

The men in Sherman's army greeted the news of the surrender at Appomattox with rampant enthusiasm and exultation. Rice C. Bull of the 123d New York Infantry recorded in his diary: "It would be impossible for me to describe the scene that followed. The men went wild, ranks were broken, and shouting and crying, the men hugged and kissed each other. Never have I witnessed such happiness. . . ."[9]

John C. Arbuckle of the Fourth Iowa Infantry observed similar reactions, writing that the men "broke forth in riotous demonstrations of joy . . . literally overcome with the thought that the war had ended."[10] George Ward Nichols, Union major and aide in Sherman's headquarters, wrote:

> This morning news of the surrender of Lee reached us. Our army went wild with excitement when this glorious result was announced. . . . Our troops gave cheer after cheer to express their joy, and then, when cheers became too feeble an expression, uttered yell upon yell until they waked the echoes for miles around. Then the bands burst forth in swelling strains of patriotic melody, which the soldiers caught up and re-echoed with their voices. Every body was proud and glad.[11]

Theodore Upson, a Union sergeant, described the scene that night as celebrations lasted into the hours of the next morning:

We had a great blow out at HD Quarters last night. . . . [General Charles Woods] had a great big bowl setting on a camp table. Evrybody was helping themselfs [*sic*] out of it. . . . After a while a Band came. They played once or twice, drank some, played some more, then drank some more of that never ending supply of punch. . . . [O]ne thing is sure: Lee has surrendered and Richmond is ours.[12]

On the morning of April 12, following breakfast, Gov. Zebulon B. Vance met at the Capitol with former governors David L. Swain and William A. Graham and composed the following letter to Sherman:

Understanding that your army is advancing on this capital, I have to request, under proper safe-conduct, a personal interview, at such time as may be agreeable to you, for the purpose of conferring upon the subject of a suspension of hostilities, with view to further communications with the authorities of the United States, touching the final termination of the existing War. If you concur in the propriety of such a proceeding I shall be obliged by an early reply.[13]

Governor Vance then appointed Swain and Graham commissioners to visit Sherman and deliver the letter. Boarding the train with Swain and Graham at 10:30 A.M. were Dr. Edward Warren, the state's surgeon general; Col. James G. Burr, an officer of the State Guard; and Maj. John Devereux of Vance's staff. The party had traveled only a short distance when the cars were halted—first by Confederate cavalry and then by Federal cavalry. Showing no respect for the state's elder statesmen, the Union soldiers took their valuables and jeered and mocked them for their appearance. Taken under guard, Vance's representatives met with Sherman and were pleased to learn that he did not intend to launch a full-scale assault against the city. The commissioners had expected to return to Governor Vance's office before the day's end; but their talks with Sherman took the better part of April 12. The general, however, would not allow them to depart and, following a meal and band serenade, provided them with sleeping quarters for the night. In the meantime Governor Vance, anticipating arrest and imprisonment, left Raleigh around midnight. In a second letter penned to Sherman before departing, Vance asked that the city's charitable institutions, the Capitol, and the state museum be spared from destruction.[14]

Gen. Judson Kilpatrick, head of Sherman's cavalry, conveyed to headquarters word that Confederates had evacuated the city and were not expected to make any stand to defend it. Sherman, evincing little of the concern for the city as stated to the commissioners, relayed back to Kilpatrick: "I don't care about Raleigh now, but want to defeat and destroy the Confederate army; therefore, you may run any risk."[15]

Union general Jacob D. Cox, among Sherman's trusted lieutenants, demonstrated more concern for the property of North Carolinians in this order, issued on April 12:

Since we left Goldsborough there has been a constant succession of house burning in the rear of this command. . . . [T]he prospect of speedy peace makes this more than ever reprehensible. Division commanders will take the most vigorous measures to put a stop to these outrages, whether committed by men of this command or by stragglers from other corps. Any one found firing a dwelling-house, or any building in close proximity to one, should be summarily shot.[16]

As the day came to a close, the rear guard of the Confederate cavalry broke into several stores and houses in downtown Raleigh. Three days later the *Daily Progress* of Raleigh included a report on the Confederate depredations. The report indicated that the soldiers carried off "what little they could find, and then wantonly [broke] up show cases, tearing down shelves and doing other damage."[17]

Surviving accounts by civilian Southerners, particularly the diaries and letters of Southern women, make palpable the fear and dread with which the arrival of Sherman's forces—particularly the "bummers"—was anticipated. The following is a firsthand account of an incident that took place in Chatham County on April 12, 1865. The date was indelibly inscribed in the memory of the writer, for it was four years to the day after the firing of the guns on Fort Sumter. Clara D. Maclean, the correspondent, was a South Carolinian living temporarily in Chatham:

> Going to the window, I looked out and saw a half-dozen horses fastened to the palings. As usual, these unwelcomed visitors had made themselves "at home," and entered by the back gate. . . .
>
> Mrs. DeG. now appeared, bathed in tears and wringing her hands pitifully. "Oh! Miss C., what shall we do? Isn't it awful?" . . .
>
> Her mother-in-law, an elderly lady—and an invalid—was lying in a small bed when the invaders arrived. They had forced her to rise, suspecting some ruse to protect valuables in or under the bedding. Then thrusting in their sabres they literally disembowelled the mattress and feather-bed, the *debris* of which was now strewn far and wide. The poor old lady was deeply distressed at the indignity of their treatment, but she opened not her lips, and surveyed the ruins with Roman fortitude. . . .
>
> The investigating Federal proceeded to open drawers and wardrobes upon reaching my room; and, after watching him a few moments, I asked quietly what he wished. . . .
>
> "Open these trunks!" . . .
>
> [Finding them empty], [h]e turned off with a horrid oath, and drawing an immense navy revolver from his boot . . . he presented it to my head. . . .
>
> But he had stationed himself in front of the door, his back toward it. For a moment, nay, a long minute—centuries it seemed to me—we stood thus. There he was, a stalwart blonde of perhaps twenty-three or four, over six feet in height; his breath hot with the peach brandy they had unearthed on this raid; his eyes blood-shot, a reckless demon looking out of their grey-green depths, ready for any atrocity. I measured him from cap to boots, then fixed my eyes steadily on his, not fearful in the least, calm to petrifaction almost, only as I pressed my left hand against my side I felt there a strange, wild fluttering, as of an imprisoned bird. With the other I slowly and stealthily unloosed the stiletto from its sheath. . . .
>
> He turned, unlocked the door, and went down, I following. . . .
>
> I saw only with divided mind the next outrage—the same man tearing open the dress-neck of the dignified old mother, and drawing thence a silk handkerchief in which was wrapped sixteen golden dollars. My blood boiled at the sight, but I dared not speak.[18]

April 13 (Thursday)

April 13 was the day Raleigh fell to Union forces and the day the war came home to citizens in the capital city and the surrounding countryside.

In Greensboro the political and military leaders of the Confederacy met again. At Pres. Jefferson Davis's request, Gen. Joseph E. Johnston contrasted the opposing armies: the Confederates' 20,000 infantry and artillery plus 5,000 cavalry versus the Union armies' combined strength of 350,000. Provisions, largely consumed or wasted by fugitives from the Army of Northern Virginia, might carry the Confederates through the end of the month. "I represented that under such circumstances it would be the greatest of human crimes for us to attempt to continue the war," Johnston later wrote. Others present, notably Secretary of State Judah P. Benjamin, counseled continuing the war. Davis reserved judgment, indicating that the Union would not negotiate and would permit only a full surrender, but authorized Johnston to meet with his counterpart, Gen. William T. Sherman. On the evening of the thirteenth, Johnston left Greensboro to rejoin his army near Hillsborough.[19]

From that date Sherman's march had importance only insofar as it led to the rapidly approaching end of the war. Skirmishing between the advance and rear guards continued, but to little if any tactical advantage. Most notable of those encounters was a rather severe skirmish between the cavalry forces of Gen. Joseph Wheeler and Gen. Judson Kilpatrick at Morrisville on April 13. Many Confederates, sensing that the end was near, lost their appetite for the fight. On the thirteenth the Fifty-fifth Illinois Volunteer Infantry Regiment captured four Confederate soldiers who were "tired of the war" and reported that Johnston's army was fast being depleted by desertions.[20]

One of the last acts of the Confederates departing Raleigh was the destruction of the railroad depot. A report on that activity appeared in a Raleigh newspaper two days later:

> The depot building of the N.C. Railroad at this place was set on fire and its contents entirely consumed early last Thursday morning [April 13]. It is said it was done by orders of the Confederate authorities. Large quantities of meat, meal, flour, &c., were burned. The building also contained bomb shells and cartridge boxes which exploded, sometimes at intervals and sometimes in rapid succession, hurling the deadly missiles in all directions. We learn that two or three persons were more or less injured, and it is almost miraculous that so little damage was done by the flying bullets and fragments of shells.[21]

The peace commissioners, having spent the night in the company of General Sherman, embarked on their return to the city with the agreement that they would notify the governor of the conditions agreed upon (they were unaware that Governor Vance had left during the night) and return to advise Sherman as to their acceptance or rejection. Five miles from the city, Kilpatrick's cavalry stopped their train but subsequently allowed it to continue under a flag of truce. As the commissioners neared the town limits, their progress was impeded by the depot fire, which could be seen from some distance. The peace commissioners' work was not uniformly welcomed. One Confederate general said, in reference to the commissioners, that they were "a couple of traitors" and ought to be hanged.[22]

Early on Thursday morning, William H. Harrison, mayor of Raleigh, accompanied by several town commissioners and other leading citizens, ventured out with a flag of truce to meet Union cavalry commander Judson Kilpatrick. Seasoned political veteran Kenneth Rayner spoke on behalf of the delegation, surrendering the city. In reply Kilpatrick stated that he intended to occupy the city and plant the flag there but that lives and property of the citizens would be protected.[23]

By 7:30 A.M. General Sherman reached the city and set up headquarters in the Governor's Palace. The streets of the city were nearly deserted. Shops were closed. At the Capitol only a servant, whom Governor Vance had entrusted with the keys to the building, remained. The Capitol's interior offered evidence of destruction committed before the arrival of the Federal troops. It was a scene of disorder, with legislative documents and maps strewn about the floor. Glass in the museum cases had been broken, and many of the specimens of natural history had been taken. The geological collections had been broken and scattered, and an inkwell had been emptied atop a defaced bust of John C. Calhoun.[24]

On the morning of the thirteenth, about a dozen Confederates, men Cornelia Phillips Spencer termed the "debris of our army," set about breaking open and plundering the stores on Fayetteville Street in Raleigh. Governor Swain, just back from his foray as a peace commissioner, observed their activities from his vantage point at the State Capitol. Swain approached the men he termed "stragglers from Wheeler's cavalry," telling them that he had assurance that Sherman's army intended that no harm would come to the city. Their response was "Damn Sherman and the town too." Another citizen, Robert G. Lewis, joined Swain in his plea that the men desist. Their exchanges, becoming more heated, were interrupted by the arrival of Kilpatrick's cavalry, whereupon the Confederates mounted their horses and left at a full gallop.[25]

One of their number, said to be a "rash young Texan" by the name of Walsh, waited until Kilpatrick's cavalry was within one hundred yards and then discharged his weapon six times in the direction of the officer at the head of the troops. He then set off, pursued by several Union soldiers. He was captured and, at the orders of Kilpatrick, hanged. Observers feared that the incident would lead to reprisals by the Union cavalry, but such did not transpire. Mrs. Spencer, in her account, described the culprit as "a vile marauder, who justly expiated his crimes, or a bold patriot, whose gallantry deserved a more generous sentence, as friend or foe shall tell his story."[26] Accounts of the incident appear in many secondary sources, but additional information as to the soldier's life and career has not been located.

Mrs. Spencer, writing within weeks of the events described, offered a rationale for the excesses and depredations committed by Confederate soldiers:

What our soldiers did or did not do in those last dark days of confusion and utter demoralization, we record with sad and tender allowance. Wrong was done in many instances, and excesses committed; but we feel that the remembrance of their high and noble qualities will in the end survive all temporary blots and blurs. And for those who perished in the wrong-doing engendered by desperation and failure and want, their cause has perished with them. So perish the memory of their faults![27]

The reputation for misdeeds gained by Wheeler's Confederate cavalry was so well known that it was the subject of jokes. Margaret Devereux of Raleigh penned this recollection in 1906:

I remember when Wheeler's cavalry passed through town that the men, when halted, just dropped in the streets and slept, so that passers-by were forced to step over them, but in spite of starvation and weariness the old indomitable spirit would assert itself. One of the poor fellows, while the column was passing by Christ Church, looked up at the weathercock and remarked to a comrade that it was the first and only instance of Wheeler's boys seeing a chicken which they could not get at.[28]

Many Union soldiers, after the war, recorded their recollections of the march. Most had memories of their time in Raleigh, where the troops were encamped from April 13 to April 29. A member of the Third Wisconsin Veteran Volunteer Infantry Regiment recalled that several men had fallen ill from sunstroke as they approached the city:

The army entered Raleigh looking shabby and dirty from its long march through the Carolinas, and the recent short battle campaign from Fayetteville to Goldsboro. The men were much in need of clothing, caps, hats and shoes. A good pair of shoes could hardly be found, while socks were a reminiscence of earlier days, consequently it was a complete transformation scene, when the men donned the new clothing recently sent from the north.[29]

Rice C. Bull of the 123d New York Infantry recalled his posting near the state asylum:

Early on the 13th, we reached Raleigh, capital of North Carolina . . . we made our camp near the State Lunatic Asylum. It was filled with demented people who rejoiced to see us, thinking that we would set them free. One of the inmates made a great plea, saying he was sane and had been placed in the asylum by the secessionists because he was a Union man. Our officers who looked into the matter found he was one of the most violent inmates in the institution. We left him there but he did make a good plea.[30]

John C. Arbuckle of the Fourth Iowa Infantry left an account of his days in Raleigh that is typical for its praise of the city and its residents:

Raleigh is an exceptionally attractive city, a city of homes, churches, situated in the midst of a rich agricultural section of the State, giving evidence of thrift and prosperity. On the whole this was one of the more inviting and attractive sections of the South through which we passed; farms were tidy and well kept. The war had not been carried into this part of North Carolina, and on our advance the people did not flee; they were in their homes, on their farms, the business of the city was not interrupted.[31]

A member of the Fifty-fifth Illinois Regiment also waxed rhapsodic about the capital city and recalled its red-carpet welcome: "Raleigh was occupied . . . and the army marching through its streets and passing in review before General Sherman at the capitol, presented a grand military pageant. Many citizens greeted it with demonstrations of joy, evincing their gratification that the close of the great conflict was near at hand. The ladies particularly were lavish with smiles and greetings of welcome, which the soldiers acknowledged by cheers as they passed."[32]

Of course, an observer's attitude toward the war and the righteousness of the Southern cause would affect his or her view of the Federal occupation. Most surviving accounts by Raleigh residents offer a stark contrast to the Union soldier's recollections. Kate McKimmon had been among the students at St. Mary's who offered food to the departing Confederate troops on April 12. Very soon after

Sherman's men moved into Raleigh, Miss McKimmon moved back to her family home downtown. She recalled: " 'Tecumseh Billie,' alias General Sherman, pitched his tent in the 'Governor's Palace.' My home was diagonally across the street, hence I had the pleasure of seeing many more 'bluecoats' than I desired. At night I was often wakened by strains of beautiful music and for a moment I would enjoy the music of silver instruments, but when I would realize the instruments were 'Yankee,' I would cover up and try not to hear."[33]

The assurances of Union commanders notwithstanding, much property in Wake County, especially outside the city of Raleigh, was destroyed during the sixteen-day occupation. Those sites included a powder mill on Crabtree Creek; Milburnie Mill, a paper mill northeast of Raleigh on the Neuse River; and Philip Thiem's machine shop in southeast Raleigh, which was set afire on the night of April 13, resulting in the loss of an engine, machinery, and tools, along with an adjacent gristmill. A paper mill at the Falls of the Neuse was reported to have been saved by the workmen, who dismantled the machinery and hid it, to be reassembled later.[34]

Foraging, on which Sherman's troops had relied for subsistence during the whole of the Carolinas Campaign, continued during their stay in Wake County. In his Special Field Order No. 55, issued shortly after his encampment in Raleigh, Sherman offered these guidelines for his troops's conduct: "No further destruction of railroads, mills, cotton, and produce, will be made without the specific orders of an army commander, and the inhabitants will be dealt with kindly, looking to an early reconciliation. The troops will be permitted, however, to gather forage and provisions as heretofore; only more care should be taken not to strip the poorer classes too closely."[35] Nonetheless, there are extensive eyewitness accounts of outrages committed by enlisted men of Sherman's army, as well as by the unregulated "bummers."

Cornelia Phillips Spencer gathered several such accounts for reprinting in her *Last Ninety Days of the War in North-Carolina*, published in 1866—initially in serial format and ultimately as a book. She prefaced the remarks with the indication that the destruction was considerably more serious in the countryside than in the city, where Union guards were posted. As an overview of the nature of the foraging, she offered these words:

> Immediately around Raleigh the farms were completely despoiled of every thing in the shape of provisions and forage, so as to leave literally nothing for the support of man or beast. In many instances the houses were burned or torn to pieces, and the fences and inclosures entirely destroyed, so as to render it impossible at that season of the year to produce one third of a crop, even with the greatest industry and attention. Every horse and mule found in the country fit for service was taken off, and only a few old and half-starved ones are to be found on the farms.[36]

Mrs. Spencer attributed the following more specific and lengthy account to an unidentified correspondent. Internal evidence indicates that the author was Charles Manly, former governor, who owned a home in town and a 1,060-acre plantation, known as "Ingleside," east of Raleigh. He wrote:

> On the thirteenth of April, General Sherman took military possession of Raleigh. A portion of his body-guard pitched their tents (eight in number) in my front-yard, which,

with a room in my office, were occupied by officers. Their servants—cook, waiters, and hostlers—took possession of my kitchens, outhouses, and stables, appropriating them in a most riotous and insolent manner. The soldiers tore down my yard and garden-fences for fuel and tents, and turned their horses and mules upon my vegetables and fruit-trees, destroying a large lot of corn, potatoes, peas, etc.; took off my horses and mules, tore off the doors, flooring, and weatherboarding of my out-houses and barns for tents; killed all my poultry, upward of thirty young hogs, cooking them in my kitchen for the officers' tables. After the removal of this squad, another took instant possession, and pitched twenty-four tents in my front-yard and a large number in the lower part of my grounds, still using my kitchen, beside building fires all over the yard. At my plantation, three miles from town, the devastation was thorough and unsparing. I had no overseer there. The negroes, some seventy in number, were plundered of their clothing and provisions, consisting of bacon, pickled beef, corn-meal, and flour. My dwelling-house was broken open, weatherboarding, flooring, and ceiling carried off, every window-sash and glass broken out, and every article of furniture for house or kitchen either carried off or wantonly destroyed. Barns, cotton-houses, and sheds were all torn down; blacksmith's, carpenter's, and farming implements carried off or broken up; three carts and two large wagons, with their gear, destroyed; the fences burned; and a large number of mules and horses pastured on the wheat-fields; all my mules and horses there (seventeen in number) carried off; fifty head of cattle, forty sheep, fifty hogs, and a large flock of geese and poultry either taken off or wantonly shot down; a quantity of medicine, some excellent wines, brandy, whisky, and two hundred gallons of vinegar were taken. Wagon-trains went down day after day, till 150 barrels of corn, 15,000 pounds of fodder, 12,000 pounds of hay, and all my wheat, peas, cotton, etc., were carried off, leaving the whole place entirely bare, so that my negroes had to come in town for rations.[37]

The Raleigh *Daily Progress* on April 15 reported that incidents of vandalism in the city were few, indicating that the store of L. H. Adams had been broken into on the night of April 13 and his safe opened and several thousand dollars in Confederate money taken. But, the editors concluded, "we have had as few outrages as could have been expected." The reason, they judged, was that "the city is well guarded, and comparative quiet prevails," since "a guard is posted at every private residence, store—in fact everywhere where desired."[38]

The newspaper's report may have been a rush to judgment in light of the firsthand account of Governor Manly, whose residences within and outside the city suffered at the hands of the occupying forces. Mrs. Spencer did not hesitate to lay the blame with the officer corps and went on to report:

A lady residing beyond the city limits, the wife of a general officer in our army, had her house repeatedly pillaged, and all the provisions belonging to her negroes, as well as her own, carried off. The tent of a general in the Federal army was pitched just in front of the house, and every marauder going in and coming out laden with spoils was immediately in his view; yet not a word was said to check the men, nor any steps allowed for her protection. A guard was refused her, on the ground of the action of Wheeler's men at their entrance; and when, after repeated solicitation, a guard reluctantly came, he allowed all who were on the premises laden, to march off with what they had in hand, saying he had no authority to take any thing away from them! The unfortunate negroes were the severest sufferers, they being literally stripped of their all, and, beginning a new life of freedom, began it without even the little savings and personal property accumulated in slavery. That General Sherman was well aware of all this, and not only tacitly permitted it, but considered it a necessary part of war that non-combatants lying at the mercy of his army should receive no mercy at all, is one of the extraordinary developments of the war. There would rather seem to be a deficiency of judgment on his part than a real want of humanity, for which he may have been indebted to the astute military training received at West-Point.

To that institution alone must be conceded the unenviable distinction of sending out soldiers instructed to carry fire, famine, and slaughter through the invaded country, and then sententiously declaring that "such is war." . . .

Even while the peace negotiations were in progress, as we have seen, and in many cases after peace was declared, the grand army hastened to improve the shining hours in Wake, Orange, and Alamance. Wholesale robbery, abuse, and insult were practiced in so many instances under the eyes of the commanding officers, that those who would have said that the officers did not know or permit such things, and that they were the work of only lawless stragglers and camp-followers, such as are found in all armies, were forced to the unavoidable conclusion that this species of warfare was encouraged and approved by the commanders as an important branch of the service, and an invaluable aid in the work of subjugation and reconstruction.[39]

Cornelia Phillips Spencer, like Charles Manly and other writers of the period, evinced a particular concern for depredations committed by Union troops against blacks. Such concern reflected a sense of paternalism, a feeling that those least able to bear the burden were nevertheless not spared the suffering. In addition, the repeated mentions of such incidents also suggest an urge to point out the irony or hypocrisy of such outrages, whereby the reputed emancipators ravage the emancipated.

Two narratives by former slaves, collected in the 1930s by interviewers working for the Federal Writers' Project, a program of the Works Progress Administration (WPA), recount experiences of young African Americans who lived in Wake County during April 1865. Patsy Mitchiner was a twelve-year-old slave in the home of newspaperman Alexander Gorman of Raleigh. She recalled being frightened by men in Wheeler's Confederate cavalry. She watched them steal garments, including "women's drawers," from the family's clothesline. The soldiers' seemingly strange behavior especially puzzled the young girl—until she saw them tie together the legs and fill the undergarments with plunder such as meat and corn, then throw the bounty across their horses' backs and ride away. Charles W. Dickens was a young slave boy on the Washington Scarborough plantation and was impressed with the "huge number" of horses, cows, and other livestock taken away by Sherman's men. He recalled that they even "stole from us slaves."[40]

Especially noteworthy are the memoirs left by several upper-class white women in Raleigh. Those memoirs more often than not concern the disruption of domestic life. Margaret Devereux's account is typical:

I cannot pretend to give you an idea of the excitement and turmoil of that last week of the Confederacy. . . . I happened to go into the dining-room and found several rough-looking men, whom I took to be Confederates, seated at supper. Robert was waiting upon them, and Adelaide talking, while one of my little children, was seated cosily upon the knee of a particularly dirty-looking man. This did not please me, for there was a freedom of manner about them which I had never seen in one of our men before. Still, I had no suspicion that they were not what they seemed, and, being called off, I left them, although a certain uncomfortable feeling caused me to do so unwillingly. Just as I left, a clatter of horses' feet was heard outside, and Adelaide (always loquacious), exclaimed, "Here come the General and his staff!'' The words were scarcely uttered before the men jumped from their seats and dashed from the room. We were afterwards convinced that they were some of the scum of Sherman's army, and while we (myself and daughters) were sitting quite unsuspectingly, they were lurking near us.[41]

For Margaret Devereux, the case of mistaken identity was one she did not intend to repeat. In another of her recollections, there was no mistaking the "bummers" and the approach of the blue-clad Federals. In the latter case the guards received special praise for the protection of her family's property:

I saw three odd, rough-looking men come galloping up from the barn. . . . They rode furiously into the yard, where they halted abruptly. The servants stood gaping at them in stupid bewilderment. I went forward and asked them the meaning of this intrusion. Their reply was an insolent demand for my keys. I knew that they were bummers. . . . I told the bummers, with a great show of courage, that I had no idea of giving them my keys, and as I walked off, feeling quite triumphant, I had the mortification of seeing them dismount and swagger to the doors of the mealroom, smokehouse, and storeroom, slip their miserable, dastardly swords into the locks, and open their doors, with the most perfect ease. Conscious now of my own weakness, I would not condescend to parley with them, and watched them at their insolent and thievish game, until their mules were almost hidden beneath the load of hams, sausages, and other plunder. They then remounted, and dashed off at the same furious pace as they had come. In a little time after others came and played the same game, only adding to their abominable thievishness by driving off our mules and all our cattle. Our horses, I am glad to say, had been sent away.

It was towards noon upon that fatal day that we espied a long blue line crawling serpent-like around a distant hill. Silently we watched, as it uncoiled itself, ever drawing nearer and still nearer, until the one great reptile developed into many reptiles and took the form of men. Men in blue tramping everywhere, horsemen careering about us with no apparent object, wagons crashing through fences as though they had been made of paper. The negroes stood like dumb things, in stupid dismay. . . .

In an incredibly short time tents were pitched, the flag run up, and the Yankees were here. The crowd grew more dense. . . . [E]very one during this period of panic entertained an idea that he must commit his valuables to the keeping of some one else. . . .

One day General [John A.] Logan came to the door and said that he had reason to believe that a Confederate officer was concealed in the house. . . . I assured him that this rumor was quite false [and] requested him to satisfy himself of the truth of my assertion by making a search of the entire house and outbuildings. I entreated him to do this, for his threats had so alarmed me that I felt that in that alone lay our preservation. His reply, with an insolent, jeering laugh, was: "I will not take that trouble, for my boys will settle that question."

The safeguards stationed both at the back and front protected the house. For, whatever might have been their feelings, they dared not relax their vigilance. The discipline in that army was perfect.[42]

Ellen Mordecai of Raleigh had little good to say about the Yankees in the following account, which practically spits invective:

No words can ever paint the bitterness, the hatred I feel for our despicable conquerors— ungenerous, lowminded, pitiful wretches. It will be just enough to say that at the hands of one or two I have had civility—I have had nothing to do *socially* with *one*. . . . For weeks before, the Yankees came, I was living in a sort of whirl. Wounded and sick Confederates in the house, and the daily administering to the wants of the passing soldiers. . . . The very day before the Yankees came in, four or five Confederates breakfasted with us. I had never seen them before, but felt as if I knew them, while I was waiting on them, and putting up the last lunch I ever gave a soldier on duty. . . .

How my blood boiled to see Yankee muskets under every window of my house! I have been annoyed . . . by the constant presence of the Yankees. My back yard does not seem to me to belong to me. Till within the last ten days, it has been a perfect thoroughfare for soldiers, Negroes and poor white folks. There was *ever* a group at the well, and soldiers hanging round my servants houses. The nuisance was intolerable. My gates were constantly open, and I dare not have them fastened—so cows were in the yard day and night. My poor little cedar hedge is a perfect wreck—my garden constantly pillaged. I was subjected to all sorts of petty annoyances and insults, and no representation of these facts to the officers produced anything but promises. . . .[43]

Some have counted Raleigh as fortunate in that there was no interval of time between the departure of the Confederates and the arrival of the Union forces, during which the "bummers" and stragglers might have run rampant. Contemporary observers were less willing to see any good fortune in their circumstances. Bartholomew Figures Moore, prominent Raleigh attorney and former attorney general of the state, is quoted as having said: "God save us from the retreating friend and advancing foe." Jonathan Worth, state treasurer and subsequently governor, spoke with northern writer J. T. Trowbridge regarding his personal experience with the "bummers." Trowbridge later wrote:

From Governor Worth, I received a rather sorry account of the doings of Sherman's "bummers" in this State. Even after the pacification they continued their lawless marauding. "They visited my place, near Raleigh, and drove off a fine flock of ewes and lambs. I was State Treasurer at the time, and having to go away on public business, I gave my negroes their bacon, which they hid behind the ceiling of the house. The Yankees came, and held an axe over the head of one of the negroes, and by threats compelled him to tell where it was. They tore off the ceiling, and stole all the bacon. They took all my cows. Three cows afterwards came back; but they recently disappeared again, and I found them in the possession of a man who says he bought them of these bummers. I had a grindstone, and as they couldn't carry it off, they smashed it. There was on my place a poor, old, blind negro woman,—the last creature in the world against whom I should suppose any person would have wished to commit a wrong. She had a new dress; and they stole even that."

"I was known as a peace man," said the Governor, "and for that reason I did not suffer as heavily as my neighbors." He gave this testimony with regard to that class which served, but did not honor, our [i.e., the Union] cause: "Of all the malignant wretches that ever cursed the earth, the hangers-on of Sherman's army were the worst;" adding: "It can't be expected that the people should love a government that has subjugated them in this way."[44]

Writing in 1877, newspaperman William R. Richardson related two instances of outrages, each the work of "bummers," that had taken place in Wake County:

A correct record of the many acts of outrage committed in the vicinity of Raleigh can never perhaps be obtained. They were in some instances, of the most horrid character, and some of the sufferers were among our most estimable citizens. Of those noted for their atrocity may be mentioned the following cases: Wesley Jones, Esq., was at the time Confederate States' Marshal, and had held the same position under the government of the United States for several years prior to the breaking out of the war. At the time of the occupation of Raleigh he was in a dying condition from a cancer of the mouth. The disease had made

— 75 —

such progress as to render him almost incapable of utterance, and he was patiently awaiting death as a happy relief from his sufferings. It was while in this pitiable condition, that a squad of "bummers" called at his residence about four miles southwest of the city. Dismounting in the yard, they inquired for Mr. Jones. They were informed of his condition and told that he could not be seen. Notwithstanding the protest and earnest entreaties of the family, they entered the house and forced their way into the dying man's chamber. With threats of the most terrible character they demanded money and other valuables. In vain did the family assure them of their utter destitution so far as money was concerned. With fiendish rage, they searched the bed on which the sufferer lay, and, amid the agonizing screams of his wife and helpless children, threatened to drag him from it, which brutal act they would have doubtless accomplished but for the earnest entreaties of an old and faithful servant. Every ounce of meal and every pound of bacon, besides everything else of an eatable character, was taken from the premises. But for the exertions of the old servant alluded to the family would have perhaps starved to death. The old man, with heroic devotion to his unfortunate master, made his way through the country to Raleigh and procured from friends the necessaries of life for the afflicted household. Mr. Jones did not for any great while, survive the ordeal. He died deeply lamented, especially by the poor and humble, to whom he ever proved himself a benefactor. . . .

Robt. Jones, Esq., . . . formerly a dry goods merchant in the city, was living at the time on his farm north of Raleigh. He was visited by a gang, who, in order to extort from him some money which it was alleged he had buried, tied a rope around his neck and led him to the barn with the avowed purpose of hoisting him up. Mr. Jones told them that he had not money, but they insisted that he had hid it, and gave as a reason for their assertion that one of the negroes had so told them . . . the old gentleman escaped bodily harm, but suffered greatly by loss of provisions.[45]

Commentators were not without an occasional word of praise for the treatment of locals at the hands of Sherman's army. Some observed how the posting of guards, in several instances, preserved personal property and merited a few words of commendation. H. C. Olive, a tobacco farmer in southwestern Wake County, writing in 1886, took just such a balanced view of the occupation:

This portion of the country had suffered by the occasional ravages of the Confederate forces which had just passed through, but the dregs of the cup were fully tested when the Sherman army arrived. . . . They were noted for their general bad behavior, and their general conduct here was not an exception. However, it is but just to say, that among them were many very noble and worthy men, but some as low and mean as the world ever knew. The only rest to be obtained by any family in this section during this time was at night. From sun rise to sun set they crowded every house, every road, lane, yard and field, without word and without ceremony, taking everything they desired, from a common brass pin to a horse or wagon, plundering most uncivilly every drawer, private room and outhouse all through the live long day, killing fine cattle (sometimes for a mess of steak), and leaving the remainder to waste. Such are some of the hardships of cruel war.[46]

Henry Hitchcock, a Union major, in his recollection of his days in Raleigh, wrote that he "had a very pleasant time in this very pretty town." Wheeler's cavalry, he wrote, "as usual, plundered the citizens, broke into stores, etc., etc., the night before." His own men, he reasoned, "behaved as well as in Savannah,—guards are stationed everywhere and on all sides we hear mingled admiration and astonishment at the good conduct, the fine appearance and condition and the soldierly bearing of our army, and the unreserved acknowledgment that the rebel cause is hopelessly 'gone up.' "[47]

Thomas Ruffin, former chief justice of the North Carolina Supreme Court and resident of both Raleigh and Hillsborough, suffered from depredations committed both by Wheeler's cavalry and by Union forces. In a letter written in August 1865 to David L. Swain, he railed against both sides:

[T]he Southern army—"Wheeler's men" . . . producing the most pungent pain & indignation because it came from those who proposed to be fighting for our protection & were doing by outrages calculated to produce in the minds of the general population the impression, that our armies consisted of lawless men, who had no regard for private rights or public faith. From them better things were to be expected while from them nothing good was to be looked for. . . . But in amount of damage that done by the Yankees far exceeded Wheeler's & was more wanton & vexatious. Between them they left me not one ear of Corn. . . . [The Yankees] shot my sheep & hogs down, which, being unfit for eating, were left to rot on the ground. . . . But the most odious loss committed is the ruin of wheat; for several thousand horses & cattle were turned on it, besides all the stock of the neighborhood for more than a week. . . . As well as I can judge the value of the plundering & burning here & devastation of crops amounts, probably, to six or seven thousand dollars. . . .[48]

Taken as a whole, the accounts of contemporary observers, Northerner and Southerner, military and civilian, placed the responsibility for the most severe depredations on the "bummers." Writing in 1877, journalist William R. Richardson anticipated the strong feelings engendered by the activities of the "bummers"—feelings that have persisted to the present: "The acts of Sherman's corps of 'bummers' did more to dissipate union sentiment in the South than all other causes combined, and the feeling of indignation and hatred engendered during the so-called 'march to the sea,' will in many cases, be transmitted from father to child, for perhaps generations to come, as legacies of ill-will towards the government of the United States."[49]

On April 13 the war came home to Raleigh and Wake County. The massive invasion by Sherman's occupying army was an event that shaped the memory of a generation and continues to reverberate in the historical consciousness 130 years later. An unidentified and virtually illiterate Confederate soldier, in a letter to his Raleigh sister published in a local newspaper on April 13, summed up the situation with respect to the war's closing days: "I hev konkludid that the dam fulishnes uv tryin to lick shurmin Had better be stoped. . . . if the dam yankees Havent got thair yit its a dam wunder. Thair thicker an lise on a hen and a dam site ornraier."[50]

April 14 (Good Friday)

April 14 will be remembered as the day John Wilkes Booth shot Pres. Abraham Lincoln at Ford's Theater. Word of the assassination on Friday evening did not reach Raleigh until the following Monday morning.

Gen. William T. Sherman issued Special Field Order No. 55 on April 14. It authorized continued reliance upon foraging for subsistence, with the stipulation that "more care should be taken not to strip the poorer classes too closely." Sherman's lieutenants reiterated the language in their instructions to their units.

C. Cadle, an officer with the Seventeenth Corps, issued the following order: "Foraging will be done by detachments in charge of the amount foraged. . . . No mills, cotton-gin presses, or produce will be destroyed without orders from these or superior headquarters. The people must be treated kindly and respected. Care must be taken in foraging to leave some provisions for families, and especial care must be taken with the poor people, not to deprive them of the means of subsistence."[51]

The issue of discipline among the men of Sherman's army is one that has drawn comment from all who have studied the closing days of the war. John G. Barrett of Virginia Military Institute, who has written most extensively on the war in North Carolina, states that "complete discipline for an army the size of Sherman's was, of course, out of the question." James M. McPherson of Princeton University, author of the best-selling *Battle Cry of Freedom*, stipulates that Sherman gained an undeserved reputation for being unprincipled and undisciplined: "[D]espite his ferocious reputation Sherman was careful with the lives of his soldiers. 'I don't want to lose men in a direct attack when it can be avoided,' he said. He would rather win by strategy and maneuver than by battle. He was confident that the war was nearly over and that his destruction of enemy resources had done much to win it. Johnston's small and demoralized force, in Sherman's view, hardly mattered any more."[52]

Nevertheless, Sherman had gained a reputation. Those Southerners whose homes and farms lay in the path of his army knew of that reputation, and it was for that reason that they went to great lengths to conceal valuables. Even among his own men, Sherman was a considerable presence. Henry Hitchcock, a Union major, wrote about the fact that Sherman was occupying the former residence of the North Carolina governor: "This is the fourth State Capitol he has walked into," Hitchcock wrote, "It's a way he has."[53]

On the morning of April 14 Sherman paid a visit to former North Carolina governor Thomas Bragg, a brother of Confederate general Braxton Bragg. On his return to headquarters he received from Kilpatrick word that Johnston was prepared to arrange a temporary suspension of hostilities. Sherman replied at once that he was willing to confer with Johnston and would keep his forces in check pending their negotiations. He suggested that they seek the same terms arranged by Grant and Lee at Appomattox:

I am fully empowered to arrange with you any terms for the suspension of further hostilities between the armies commanded by you and those commanded by myself, and will be willing to confer with you to that end. I will limit the advance of my main column, to-morrow, to Morrisville, and the cavalry to the university, and expect that you will also maintain the present position of your forces until each has notice of a failure to agree.

That a basis of action may be had, I undertake to abide by the same terms and conditions as were made by Generals Grant and Lee at Appomattox Court-House, on the 9th instant, relative to our two armies; and, furthermore, to obtain from General Grant an order to suspend the movements of any troops from the direction of Virginia. General Stoneman is under my command, and my order will suspend any devastation or destruction contemplated by him. I will add that I really desire to save the people of North Carolina the damage they would sustain by the march of this army through the central or western parts of the State.[54]

To facilitate the travel of Sherman and fellow officers to meet with their Confederate counterparts, a special train was sent along the tracks to Morrisville. Fearing that torpedoes might disrupt the caravan, the officer in charge of the arrangements placed several cars ahead of the locomotive to explode any such charges.[55]

In his letter to Johnston, Sherman referred to his intention to hold the cavalry forces at the university. On the fourteenth, Confederate general Joseph Wheeler moved his cavalrymen to points near Chapel Hill. That evening, at the Atkins plantation on rain-swollen New Hope Creek eight miles east of the village, the cavalry forces clashed. Wheeler's men destroyed the bridge across the creek, forcing their opponents to cross on fallen trees and driftwood. Several men on both sides were killed. But by day's end, Kilpatrick's Union cavalry, positioned just outside Chapel Hill, was set to move forward.[56]

April 15 (Saturday)

On April 15 President Lincoln died from the wounds suffered at the hands of his assassin the previous night. Raleigh native Andrew Johnson was sworn into office as president of the United States. Jefferson Davis, having authorized negotiations by General Johnston, departed Greensboro with a cavalry escort. Some officials were on horseback, and some were in carriages or wagons. Governor Vance decided to obey President Davis's summons before accepting General Sherman's invitation to meet him in Raleigh. Vance missed the appointment with Davis, remaining with General Johnston in Hillsborough for the duration of the peace talks, and eventually met with Davis in Charlotte.[57]

The scene at Sherman's headquarters in Raleigh, where it rained most of the day, was relatively peaceful. Maj. Henry Hitchcock, Sherman's aide, anticipated the events of the coming days:

> So it seems likely, at this present writing, that we may be in Raleigh for some time yet. If like terms are made with Johnston to those made with Lee, complete muster-rolls of J.'s army will have to be made out and signed in duplicate, arms, ammunitions, stores, etc., etc., transferred; and to do all this will no doubt occupy at least a fortnight. After that, I suppose this army or the greater part of it will very likely march northwards—but 'tis no use to speculate. . . . It has been raining nearly all day. . . . I am already tired out with lounging around the house with nothing to do but help entertain the officers who come to Headquarters.[58]

The sense of dread and anticipation had spread to towns in the outlying area. Anna Fuller lived in Louisburg, seat of Franklin County, about forty miles northeast of Raleigh. She wrote:

> I have not the language to depict the horrors of the past four or five days. The gloom and *despondency* that hang around everything is o'er whelming. We are almost, a conquered people, at least, we are overpowered. . . . Gen. Lee surrendered . . . last Sunday (9th). . . . The rest of the army is scattered in every direction. The enemy now is in hot pursuit after Gen. Johns[t]on, and it is seriously apprehended, that he too will surrender.

For the last three days we have been hourly expecting the Yankees here—servants reported them at Franklinton—We looked and listened all day. Almost every sound startled me.[59]

W. H. Pleasants, mayor of Louisburg, took the initiative and formally surrendered the town to General Sherman, requesting the posting of guards to safeguard property. Anna Fuller's husband, Jones, a cotton broker and merchant, was part of the delegation that delivered this message:

> In accordance with a resolution passed by the Board of Commissioners of the town of Louisburg, N.C., I hereby formally surrender this place to the authorities of the United States, and in behalf of our citizens desire and request that you will be pleased to send us a guard under a proper officer, to be stationed here, so as to preserve order and afford us that protection which under existing circumstances we feel authorized to claim under the Constitution and laws of the United States. Should you be good enough to comply with our wishes in this respect you may be well assured of our united co-operation. Messrs. J. Fuller and Dr. E. Malone are deputed as the bearers of this communication.[60]

Tradition has it that General Sherman's immediate response to the mayor's plea was "Louisburg—hell—what and where is it?" The formal response, which may or may not have been reassuring, was as follows:

> Your communication of this date is received. It is not my present intention to move any part of this army through Louisburg, and I do not think you will be molested in any manner; nor can I send a small detachment, because it would be exposed to danger from Hampton's cavalry. But I think I can promise you that events are in progress that will soon give peace to all the good people of North Carolina. Mr. William A. Graham, of Hillsborough, has gone to Governor Vance to assure him that he has my full promise of assistance of protection if he will return and maintain good order in the State. I am also now in correspondence with General Johnston, which I hope will result in an universal peace. The gentlemen who bear this letter can explain many things that will, I hope, tend to allay any fears occasioned by the falsehoods circulated by the rebel cavalry.[61]

Although little of consequence was happening in Raleigh and Greensboro, such was not the case in other parts of the state. Capt. W. E. Stoney was part of Johnson Hagood's brigade, a Confederate unit made up mostly of South Carolinians. Posted on the Haw River southeast of Greensboro, the outfit experienced difficulties in moving about, aggravated by the day's heavy rain. Captain Stoney recorded this vivid scene in his diary:

Early in the day encountered the Haw River swollen with a freshet; crossed with much difficulty but no loss; a few men were washed away by the current but not drowned. Three miles beyond the river the direction of the march was changed to Salisbury. On this road a mill stream was encountered, about twenty feet wide, but so rapid and deep that the wagons were gotten over with difficulty. The Allemance [Alamance Creek], out of its banks, next crossed our path. A few men succeeded in crossing by *chaining their hands* or by holding on to horses' tails of the mounted men, who half waded, half swam over, but the wagons were at a hopeless standstill. General Hardee was on the farther bank, evidently anxious for rapid movement and nonplussed by the obstacle. At length the leading teamster was ordered to attempt the passage. With a crack of the whip, and a shout to his mules he is in and under, rises, struggles, and is swept away. Everything was again at a standstill; the rain was falling in torrents, the river was rapidly rising, something had to be done, and our lieutenant-general determined to try to swim another wagon and team across. The order was given, and followed by the same result. Mules, wagon and teamster were swept down the stream; and it was hard to tell which was uppermost in the struggle with the flood. The general's resources seemed now exhausted and he ordered the destruction of the train. General Hoke suggested a more practicable crossing might be found, and he was permitted to seek it. Four miles higher up we crossed without difficulty at Holt's mill, and the train was saved. Encamped half a mile beyond the river after a most fatiguing day's march. Tonight, Colonel Olmstead, of the First Georgia regiment, tells me positively that *General Lee has surrendered.* Great God! can it be true? I have never for a moment doubted the ultimate success of our cause. I cannot believe it.[62]

April 16 (Easter Sunday)

On Easter Sunday, April 16, Sherman and Johnston set their plans for a conference to end hostilities. With improved weather, Kilpatrick's cavalry moved into Chapel Hill toward day's end. President Davis's party continued its southward flight, arriving at Lexington, North Carolina, and moved on rapidly toward Charlotte.

Johnston and Sherman agreed to meet at some point between Durham and Hillsborough, or approximately midway between their armies in Greensboro and Raleigh.[63] Johnston's army, on April 16 and continuing through the rest of the month, began to gather in an encampment about a mile east of the center of Greensboro near the present location of North Carolina A & T State University. Johnston's own headquarters were some distance away, near the present campus of the University of North Carolina at Greensboro. Like Raleigh, Greensboro was transformed by the presence of the army. Johnston's men swamped the little village of about eighteen hundred people.[64]

After the fall of Richmond, Confederate stores were transferred from that city to Greensboro. Rioting Confederate soldiers, deserters, and stragglers raided the army and navy supplies. Cavalry used armed force to defend the stores. Confederate rear admiral Raphael Semmes witnessed on April 16 outside Greensboro "a stream of vagabonds—some Lee's men—many deserters who are seizing horses, & otherwise robbing & plundering."[65] Just two days earlier, Gen. P. G. T. Beauregard had called upon Gen. G. G. Dibrell, commander of a division of Tennessee cavalry, to answer for his men's having "commenced an attack on the public stores" near Greensboro.[66] On April 15, according to the diary of Confederate soldier Joseph Mullen Jr.: "Wheeler's Cavalry *charged* the commissary. Off we went in double quick time. As we rushed up and ordered them to disperse, some few of them wheeled, drew their pistols and fired upon us, but without hurting anybody. We immediately turned the fire with a better effect than they had. We killed two men and one horse and wounded one other man. They then took flight, running off at the quickest possible speed in every direction."[67]

The problem of Confederate plundering was not confined to Greensboro. On April 16 Governor Vance wrote to General Johnston to complain that "stores of leather blankets &c. at Graham were pillaged and I confess I am getting tired of it." R. C. Gatlin from Johnston's headquarters had been assigned on April 13 to investigate the situation. Officers on the scene told Gatlin of their fears that "stragglers from Lee's Army" would further raid the supplies. Gatlin agreed to transport seven thousand pairs of pants back to Greensboro but could not take responsibility for the blankets and leather. When Gatlin arrived in Greensboro on April 15, he reported that "a mob of citizens and soldiers crowded the streets laden with shoes[,] cloth & clothing." Within days Governor Vance complained to Johnston of the potential at Company Shops for attacks on the rail cars carrying the archives and funds of the state treasury. Johnston ordered that guards be posted on April 19 to safeguard against such an attack.[68]

Confederate attacks and plundering of supplies have not received the attention from historians due the subject. Ethel Stephens Arnett of Greensboro, author of *Confederate Guns Were Stacked, Greensboro, North Carolina*, placed little blame on Confederate troops but quoted Letitia Morehead Walker of Greensboro, daughter of Gov. John Motley Morehead, who recalled that the supplies were distributed to sick and returning soldiers until the surrender of the army became a fait accompli. Then the distribution system fell apart and, in order to prevent the capture of the supplies by Federal troops, the lots, according to Arnett, were turned over to soldiers and civilians.[69] In any event, because of the loss of the stores, Johnston shortly would be forced to turn to Sherman for supplies to prevent his men from starving on their way back home.

Residents of Chapel Hill awoke to a beautiful Easter Sunday morning. All were prepared for the imminent arrival of the Union troops. Prof. Charles Phillips had hidden the family silver in a horseradish bed. Judge W. H. Battle buried his silver service under a maple tree near his home, only to forget later which one. Others placed their treasures in wells. Late in the afternoon university president David L. Swain, who had just returned from his service as a peace commissioner in Raleigh, several times proceeded first down the Durham road and then down the Raleigh road with a white handkerchief tied to a pole as a flag of truce. He failed to encounter the intruders but eventually, about sunset, twenty blue-clad cavalrymen led by Capt. J. M. Schermerhorn of the Ninety-second Illinois Cavalry Regiment rode into the village. The officer informed Swain that he had orders to protect the university.[70]

Among the most familiar incidents associated with the closing days of the war in North Carolina is the courtship and subsequent marriage of Swain's daughter, Eleanor, to Gen. Smith D. Atkins, commander of the Union soldiers occupying Chapel Hill. The troops generally received plaudits for their work in protecting town and campus. Guards were readily posted at each residence. After the war Cornelia Phillips Spencer had many long conversations with General Atkins. He told her that he would be willing to return to any house where he was quartered while in North Carolina and that he would be assured of receiving a courteous welcome. He asserted that his own brigade, with a single exception, did its best to prevent plundering and to protect the people. He admitted that there was little or no discipline in Sherman's army and said that it was impossible to enforce it.[71]

Jones Fuller returned home to his wife in Louisburg from his meeting with Sherman. With him he brought the promise of protection. Anna Fuller remained skeptical. In her diary, she noted that Sherman had given her husband's party "a 'safe conduct,' for themselves and horses out of the Yankee lines; but they were scarcely out of the corporate limits, before they were arrested by one of them, and their horses demanded."[72]

North Carolina's best-known diarist during the Civil War era, Catherine Edmondston, lived in Halifax County, northeast of Louisburg. The "Secesh Lady," as she styled herself, recorded on April 16 that Sherman's troops had entered Raleigh the previous week and that "rumour has it that they committed no excesses." She remained dubious, however, and expected the worst, "so little faith have I in his wolves."[73]

April 17 (Monday)

April 17 marked the first meeting between Sherman and Johnston, which took place near Durham's Station (present Durham) at the farmstead of James and Nancy Bennitt (the site subsequently became known as the Bennett Place). News of the death of President Lincoln reached North Carolina, exciting concern about the impact on the talks and the possibility of retribution against Tar Heels by Union troops. Jefferson Davis and his party were at Salisbury en route to Charlotte.

Rumors of the pending surrender by this time had reached most Confederate units, leading to widespread demoralization and disarray. Desertions became more common, and supplies were regularly plundered. Capt. W. E. Stoney of Johnson Hagood's brigade of South Carolinians, posted outside Greensboro, recorded in his diary:

Early in the day it was reported *our army* was to be surrendered. This rumor was at first disregarded, but presently began to assume shape and force. The wildest excitement seized the troops. . . . Colonel Rion immediately ordered the brigade into line and urged them not to leave. The enemy were now supposed to be not only in rear, but on both flanks, and it would be difficult to escape; that if any considerable number left it might compromise the terms given to those that remained. The men seemed at this time ready to do anything that their officers advised, to march that night in the effort to cut their way out, or to remain and abide the issue where they were. All the afternoon the cavalry were passing us saying they "were going out." The infantry soon became almost frantic, and in every direction were rushing to beg, borrow, buy and steal horses. Disorganization was complete. Horses and mules were everywhere taken without the least regard to ownership. Trains were openly carried off after plundering the wagons. The division supply train was thoroughly stripped. The flags of the brigade were burned by the men in the certainty of surrender. About dark an order came from army headquarters to keep the men together, but with that day the army perished—a mob remained.[74]

Confederate rear admiral Raphael Semmes recorded in his diary that "all the public stores ha[d] been plundered the day before," adding that "the vultures [are] scouting their prey for ten miles around."[75]

Just as Sherman prepared to enter the rail car to depart Raleigh for the talks, he was halted by a telegraph operator, who at that moment was receiving an urgent coded message for the general. For thirty minutes the train stood still. The message, from Secretary of War Edwin Stanton, announced the death of the president. Sherman swore the operator to secrecy and boarded the train.[76]

About ten o'clock in the morning Sherman and his party reached Durham's Station, where Kilpatrick had assembled a squadron of cavalry to receive them. A brief search for available quarters for their talks led them to the farmhouse of James Bennitt, who readily offered up his home for that purpose. David P. Conyngham, a correspondent for the *New York Herald* and witness to the scene, described the principals and two hot-headed members of their officer corps:

General Sherman smoked his cigar, had his hands stuffed in his pockets, as usual—on the whole, looked at ease, and perfectly the master of the situation.

Johnston, on the other hand, was taciturn, and looked haggard and care-worn, but still maintained the dignity of the soldier and the gentleman, as he certainly is.

Wade Hampton looked savage enough to eat little Kil [Judson Kilpatrick], with a grain of salt; while the latter returned his looks most defiantly.

It was evident that they would break out. At length Hampton taunted Kil about his recent surprise of his camp. . . .

Words grew hot,—both parties expressing a desire that the issue of the war would be left between their cavalry. The affair was becoming too personal; so Sherman and Johnston had to interfere.[77]

As soon as they were alone together, Sherman shared with Johnston the dispatch announcing Lincoln's assassination. According to Sherman's account, beads of perspiration broke out on Johnston's forehead, and he denounced the act as "a disgrace to the age," disavowing any connection with the Confederate government. Sherman voiced his view that he would not expect involvement in a plot by General Lee or officers of the army but that he could not be as certain about Jeff Davis or "men of that stripe." Sherman's greatest fear was that "some foolish woman or man in Raleigh might say something or do something that would madden our men, and that a fate worse than that of Columbia would befall the place."[78] Sherman and Johnston discussed the preliminary terms for an end to hostilities and agreed to meet again the following day.

That night, from his headquarters in Raleigh, Sherman announced Lincoln's death in his Special Field Order No. 56. Before having the order published and distributed, General Sherman drew up special instructions for Gen. Jacob D. Cox, whose forces garrisoned the city of Raleigh. Those instructions further strengthened the safeguards and enforced security at all roads leading from outlying encampments into the city. The coupling of the assassination news with that of the first day's truce talks helped blunt the shock and may have spared North Carolina's capital the fate of its neighbor to the south.[79]

Most officers were able to keep their men in camp as ordered that evening. Nevertheless, a band of stragglers set out from a point southwest of town toward the Capitol, torches in hand. The men turned back only when Gen. John A. Logan confronted them and threatened to shoot anyone who did not return immediately to his post.[80]

Accounts left by Northern officers reveal the depth of feeling stirred by Lincoln's death. Henry J. Aten of the Eighty-fifth Illinois Infantry recalled:

Up to this hour the only desire of the men had been to end the war and go home. To that end they had been willing to undertake any hardship, endure every privation, and brave any danger. But now that one so gentle, so kind and forgiving, should be so causelessly murdered seemed incomprehensible, and they began instinctively to lay this monstrous crime to the brutalizing influence of a system that had debauched the people of the South and to regard it as a legitimate consequence of rebellion against lawful authority. Then a desire for vengeance took possession of them, and they rejoiced in the thought that negotiations for surrender might fail, that hostilitites might be resumed. . . . But this terrible desire for vengeance passed away; the avenging hand was stayed, and neither shot nor shell was sent on its deadly mission.[81]

An Ohio private later wrote about receipt of the news: "[I]f this army had gone on another campaign I should pity the rebels that we met and the country through which we passed. For every man would take it upon himself to do every thing he could to avenge the death of old Abe, and dearly he would have been avenged for the boys would have shown no mercy."[82]

On the evening of the seventeenth and the morning of the eighteenth, Sherman met with the officers of his army (Schofield, Slocum, Howard, Logan, Blair), and to a man they advised him to agree to terms at the pending resumption of talks with Johnston. All dreaded a long and frustrating march in pursuit of a dissolving and fleeing army. "We all knew that if we could bring Johnston's army to bay, we could destroy it in an hour, but that was simply impossible in the country in which we found ourselves," Sherman wrote.[83]

George Ward Nichols, a Union major, summarized the importance of the day's events:

The day of this conference—Monday, April 17th—will be memorable in the history of the war. The fratricidal struggle of four long and weary years virtually ended on the day when two great men came together in the heart of the State of North Carolina, intent, with true nobility of soul and in the highest interests of humanity, upon putting a stop to the needless sacrifice of life. . . . The scene was symbolic of the new era of peace then just beginning to dawn upon the nation.[84]

The contrast with the mood in the Confederate camps was stark. Bromfield L. Ridley, an officer with the Army of Tennessee, wrote on April 17: "Gloom and sadness pervades the whole land; subjugation stares us in the face. Our Army of Tennessee (so called after the permanent organization at Smithfield), now has to cope with Grant, Sherman, and Thomas. If we pass through the states of South Carolina, Georgia, Alabama, and Mississippi, we will have no army. What can we do? Oh, the humility attending submission!"[85] Confederate captain W. E. Stoney wrote that "demoralization . . . is utter and complete; there is no spark of fight in the troops," adding "Our remaining supplies of commissary and quartermaster stores are fully issued, but forage for the animals is failing."[86]

In Raleigh and Wake County, foraging for supplies by Union troops continued. Elizabeth Reid Murray, historian of Wake County, points out that examples exist to prove that in some instances the Union army paid or issued receipts for goods received. On April 17 Lieut. L. T. Lucas handed Miss Betsy Hinton of Clay Hill plantation a note that read: "I have this day received of Mrs. E. Hinton 50 bushels of shelled corn for the use of the 1st Engrs., Mo. Vols."[87]

As of late evening on April 16, only a handful of Union cavalrymen had moved into Chapel Hill. The next morning a detachment under Gen. Smith D. Atkins, four thousand strong, entered the village at about 8:00 A.M. Guards were immediately posted at each house. Cornelia Phillips Spencer indicated that isolated instances of depredations took place. Just outside town a squad of "bummers" entered a house, and "in less than ten minutes the lower rooms, store-rooms, and bed-rooms were overhauled and plundered with a swift and business-like thoroughness only attainable by long and extensive practice." The guards soon arrived, but the plunder was not restored. Mrs. Spencer in particular commended the Ninth Michigan Cavalry "as being a decent set of men, while they were here, behav[ing] with civility and propriety."[88]

April 18 (Tuesday)

On April 18, as the body of Abraham Lincoln lay in state in the East Room of the White House, Jefferson Davis and his party slowly moved southward to Concord. Sherman and Johnston met at the Bennitt farmhouse for a second day. The meeting commenced punctually at noon. Both Sherman in his *Memoirs* and Johnston in his *Narrative* give accounts of the afternoon's negotiations. The versions are remarkable for their similarities. Only on minor points do they vary. The culmination of the talks was the signing of a "Memorandum or Basis of Agreement." That document, to be the subject of much criticism directed toward Sherman personally in coming days, called for an armistice by all armies in the field. Confederate forces were to be disbanded, and soldiers were to deposit their arms in state arsenals. Each soldier was to agree to cease from war and to abide by state and federal authority. The president of the United States would recognize the existing state governments when their officials took oaths to the United States. Federal courts would be reestablished. People would be guaranteed rights of person and property. The United States would not disturb the people of the South so long as they lived in peace. The plan further called for a general amnesty for Confederates.[89] In coming to those agreements, the two generals went far beyond the work of Lee and Grant at Appomattox in setting up a political framework for the postwar period.

That night Sherman wrote to Generals Ulysses Grant and Henry Halleck, outlining the plan. The terms backed by Sherman and readily agreed to by Johnston would create a firestorm of controversy in the coming days. Northern newspapers denounced Sherman for being a traitor to the cause for which he had fought. Members of the late president's cabinet, notably Edwin Stanton, questioned Sherman's wisdom and reliability. Sherman denied vociferously any usurpation of power on his part and argued that the arrangements were a product of his understanding of President Lincoln's wishes as conveyed to him at their City Point conference.

Not surprisingly, Southerners were pleased with the terms. Pres. Jefferson Davis gave them his approval as soon as he learned of them. Cornelia Phillips Spencer had relatively kind words to say about Sherman and his plan for the South. She wrote:

In however unfavorable light strict regard for the truth of history places General Sherman as a disciplinarian and leader of the great army which swept the Southern States with a besom of destruction; however dark the pictures of lawless pillage and brutal outrage, unrestrained and uncensured by the Commanding General—if indeed they were not especially directed and approved by him and his officers; however unenviable General Sherman's fame in *these* respects, equal regard for truth demands that in representing him at the council-board he shall appear in a much more commendable aspect, exhibiting there feelings of humanity and a capacity for enlarged and generous statesmanship entirely worthy of a really great general. If General Sherman's views and plans for closing the war had been adopted by his government, there can be no doubt that peace would have been *accomplished* in less than two months from the surrender of our armies; peace that would have been speedily followed by goodwill in every Southern State, in spite of the waste and burning track of his army.[90]

Historians have debated the merits of Sherman's original plan and his motives for seeking relatively lenient terms. John G. Barrett has argued that Sherman's actions were motivated by his "controlling passion to reunite the Union and at the same time aid the South."[91] Recent Sherman biographer John F. Marszalek contends that the plan was consistent with Sherman's views:

He had regularly said throughout the war that once Southerners stopped fighting and admitted their mistake, the conflict could end, and they could return to the Union with no questions asked. He viewed the enemy as fallen-away friends who needed chastisement to find their way back but no further punishment. In his single-minded determination to wage this kind of war, he did not understand that most others believed punishment was precisely what the recalcitrant South needed to ensure no future repetition of nation breaking. There was a great deal of animosity toward the South in the nation, and Sherman's leniency seemed shocking.[92]

At any rate, the war had now come to an end in the Carolinas, Georgia, and Florida as a consequence of the actions of Sherman and Johnston at the Bennitt farmhouse.

April 19 (Wednesday)

On the day that funeral services were held for President Lincoln, President Davis and his entourage, escorted by one of Wheeler's brigades, arrived in Charlotte, where they would remain for one week. Suitable quarters were difficult to find. Mrs. Davis had been in Charlotte for several weeks.

In Raleigh, Sherman wired authorities in Morehead City to prepare a steamer to carry a messenger to Washington to convey the news of his talks with Johnston. Late in the day Sherman informed his troops of the armistice. Predictably, news of the peace produced widely varying responses among the troops on the two sides. Charles W. Wills, an Illinois officer, wrote on the nineteenth: "Joe Johnston surrendered the whole thing yesterday to Sherman. Our 4th division and a division of the 17th Corps receive the arms, etc. We go into a regular camp tomorrow to await developments. If any more Confederacy crops out, we, I suppose, will go for it, otherwise in a couple of months we'll muster out. Good bye, war."[93] Thomas Ward Osborn of New York, bivouacked in Raleigh, wrote these lines in his diary:

The war is over. General Johnston, approved by General Breckinridge, Confederate Secretary of War, last evening surrendered all the enemy's forces. . . .

Could we have imagined, a few weeks ago, that it was possible for the Confederacy to have collapsed so suddenly and effectually. . . .

General Johnston yesterday told General Sherman that this Army was the best and most perfectly organized Army that ever existed, that history speaks of nothing like it since the days of Julius Caesar. . . . [I]t has been with considerable difficulty that the Army has been restrained from acts of revenge. It was necessary to guard the city two days to prevent its destruction, but all is quiet now and there will be no trouble. The discipline of this Army has certainly come to the aid of the people of Raleigh just at this time.

This is a beautiful city of 6,000 or 7,000 people. No damage has been done it.[94]

In Greensboro the armistice produced a great sense of uneasiness among the encamped Confederates, many of whom believed that the terms of surrender would ultimately lead to the taking of prisoners of war. That apprehension caused a great many desertions between April 19 and April 26, estimated by General Johnston to have been no fewer than four thousand men from the infantry and a similar number from the cavalry. Many soldiers rode off with artillery horses or mules belonging to supply trains.[95] "Our army is getting demoralized," wrote Confederate officer Bromfield L. Ridley, who added: "[A] band of marauding soldiers visited our camp this morning and coolly helped themselves to some leather and goods that we had quietly secured from the Quartermaster's Department."[96]

General Johnston made arrangements to divide among the remaining soldiers thirty-nine thousand dollars in silver. In doing so he disobeyed the instruction of President Davis that the money be sent to him at Charlotte, reasoning that "only the military part of our Government had then any existence."[97]

April 20 (Thursday)

April 20 marked a milestone for the Union forces in Raleigh: one week in the capital city. In the morning Sherman dispatched Maj. Henry Hitchcock to Washington, reckoning that the round trip would require four or five days. The Union troops spent the week making repairs to railroad and telegraph lines. Sherman himself devoted much time to reviewing his troops. On the twentieth he inspected the Tenth Corps, which included a division of black troops—the "first I had ever seen as part of an organized army"—and pronounced himself "much pleased at the[ir] appearance."[98]

Relations between citizens of Wake and surrounding counties and the Union soldiers had improved only marginally in a week's time. John G. Barrett writes that there was "very little open hostility between the soldiers and the citizens of Raleigh," contending that "the men in blue seemed to have made a conscientious effort to conciliate rather than antagonize the inhabitants." Sherman observed that Raleigh was "full of fine people who were secesh but now are willing to encourage the visits of handsome men."[99]

Foraging continued, although some officers, aware that many of the farms had been stripped of their stock and provisions, issued stricter orders with respect to gathering subsistence supplies. Gen. O. O. Howard was so disturbed by the reports of depredations that he ordered that no more animals or stores were to be taken without specific orders from division or corps commanders. The Fifty-fifth Illinois Regiment came up with a novel approach for procuring supplies:

> While in camp about four miles north of Raleigh . . . during the delay attending the arrangement of the terms of surrender for Johnston's army, the men who for a time had been subsisting exclusively upon the rations furnished by government, began to weary of their monotonous diet. They had for so many months been feasting upon the fat of the land that hard-bread and salt pork palled upon their appetites. Foraging was, however, positively forbidden by order, early in April. The situation seemed to veterans to warrant the adoption of extraordinary and perhaps even questionable measures. A squad of men from the regiment went out about ten miles to a wealthy planter's and persuaded him to sell them a wagon-load of miscellaneous provisions, *very cheap*. He was permitted to accompany them to camp in order to convey the purchase with his own team and wagon, but was mildly enjoined to reply promptly to any inquirers who might ask impertinent questions about his load, that the soldiers had satisfactorily paid for it. This he did, the goods were safely delivered, and the expedition was proclaimed a glorious success.[100]

With respect to foraging, the stay in Wake County amounted to a feast after the famine. "On the whole campaign the men had to live on the country," wrote Edward S. Salomon of the Eighty-second Illinois Infantry, "most of the time plenty of forage was obtained, but a portion of the country we marched through was very poor, and the men could hardly get as much as they needed."[101]

With an almost total breakdown in discipline and authority near supply trains, some Confederate soldiers took the law into their hands. On April 20 Governor Vance again wrote to Johnston to complain of unrestrained plunder of supplies by Confederate troops:

> Capt. Oliver, Qr. Master at Graham N.C. reports that he delivered under pressure of the mob of soldiers 6300 pairs of pants 7000 cts. of leather, 21 bales Blankets (100 to the bale)[,] ten coils Rope & 2000 yds. of Jeans Cloth. There was actually taken by the mob 5000 cts. leather, & 3000 yrs. cloth, in which the citizens participated. In addition to these statements of my Qr. Master I myself saw the conclusion of the sacking of a train at McLeans Station yesterday morning by Soldiers laden with blankets & leather. The Cars had just been emptied as I got there and the road side [was] crowded with soldiers staggering under heavy loads of the plunder. It seemed to be understood & permitted matter as officers of nearly all grades were standing quietly around. . . .[102]

Quartermaster James Sloan on April 20 wrote Governor Vance about the loss of supplies at Graham—that is, at Company Shops on the North Carolina Railroad. He credited the work of his "untiring assistants" on the scene "under circumstances of the most embarrassing and unpleasant character" with preventing further loss. Sloan noted that

> The raid on my office & ware houses, on Saturday last (i.e., April 15), resulted in the destruction of my personal effects, Books, papers some 1200 to 1500 lbs. English & Domestic upper & sole leather, & some three hundred Pair Shoes (300) &c. & a quantity of cloth Clothing & Blankets.
>
> The destruction of my books vouchers &c. is irreparable. At the time it occured, a heavy rain was falling, streets very muddy, Papers, books &c. trodden under foot of man &

beast, and the raid was not quelled untill a squad of a few men from the 7th N.C. Regt. fired on the mob, Killing One, & mortally wounding some three others.[103]

Depredations were not limited to Wake County or to points along the North Carolina Railroad. Surrounding areas were also affected. Catherine Edmondston of Halifax County, relatively isolated from the events of consequence in the closing days of the war, recorded in her diary on April 20 an incident involving the theft of horses by Union troops and their return: "It seems that the return of our impressed horses is due not to the wisdom of the Impressing Officers, but to the energy of our fellow citizens who knowing the impossibility of their getting thro the Yankee lines, followed them & forced them at the pistol's point to surrender them, but not before they had made way with & lost large numbers of them. They actually swapped one animal off for some whisky or rather Apple Brandy, for that is the country drink now. . . ."[104]

Another female diarist, Anna Fuller of Louisburg, continued to fret over the approach of the Yankees: "We were dreadfully frightened, running hither and thither, collecting scattered clothes. I made Atlas [a slave] take my box of silver, and go with it I do not know where. The Servants were much frightened too. . . ."[105]

April 21 (Friday)

Sherman continued to review the troops in Raleigh. The days in camp had enabled the soldiers to scrub up and create their best appearance. A published history of the Third Wisconsin Regiment offers this assessment: "[T]he men came out again in uniform, with closely cropped hair, cleanly shaved faces, arms and accoutrements cleaned and polished, looking as fresh, smart and tidy as militia. The newly issued 'pup' tents were again erected and the camps had the order, regularity and neatness of by-gone days. The men revelled in rest, cleanliness and wholesome rations, properly cooked, and best of all, were allowed plenty of time to eat their food."[106]

While Johnston's troops awaited their mustering-out near Greensboro, men from Lee's army in Virginia poured through the Tar Heel State en route to points further south. On April 21 a soldier of the Fifteenth Illinois Infantry, posted near Goldsboro, offered this observation on the parolees and on the consequences of the war: "We are now continually passing paroled men from Lee's army on their way to their homes, or to where their homes were. Many found blackened ruins instead, and kindred and friends gone, they knew not whither. Oh, how much misery treason and rebellion have brought upon our land!"[107]

In many instances an official record, a diary entry, or a quotation from a soldier's letter of the period can raise as many questions as it answers. This is the case with a dispatch written from Durham's Station on April 21, 1865, by L. M. Dayton, an assistant to General Sherman. The note to Gen. Judson Kilpatrick read in full: "Drum out the man who committed the rape of the negro woman and you will have the sanction of the General." Instances of rape during the course of Sherman's march were rarely reported—which makes this document in the National Archives all the more remarkable.[108]

April 22 (Saturday)

Rice C. Bull of the 123d New York Infantry recorded in his diary that "on April 22nd we were reviewed by General Sherman after we had marched through the streets of Raleigh."[109]

Jonathan Worth, writing from Company Shops on April 22 to his brother, Addison, commented on the depredations of Wheeler's men: "Our Cavalry are apparently without discipline—the terror of every body as far as I can hear, who has a horse or a mule within twenty miles of the line of march." With respect to personal losses suffered at the hands of Sherman's troops, Worth wrote that "I have no doubt that my family and property at Raleigh is all safe—but I fear that I have lost my teams, wheat at Pittsboro, and cotton in Anson."[110]

On April 22 Confederate officer Bromfield L. Ridley heard of the plans to compensate his soldiers upon mustering out: "I learn from a staff officer of General Johnston (Major Clarke), that orders are being issued to divide with the army all the silver coins in possession of Johnston's paymaster—$54,000. This will give each man $1.80, a small sum for four years' trials and hardships, and pain, and loss of treasures, blood and life."[111]

General Johnston on April 22 wrote John Breckinridge, secretary of war of the Confederacy, to apprise him of the situation with respect to supplies, noting that "large amounts have been taken violently." Johnston relayed a letter from Governor Vance that discussed the loss of state items. Vance concluded his letter with these words: "As there remains no one to whom we can look for payment in the future, and as it bears peculiarly hard upon North Carolina, to be compelled alone to pay the debts in Europe contracted for the purchase of the most of these articles which have inured to the common [illegible] of all the States, I am exceedingly anxious to know if some arrangement cannot be made by which in part the state may be indemnified."[112]

April 23 (Sunday)

On April 23 Confederate president Jefferson Davis, still quartered in Charlotte, reflected on the events of the past several weeks: "Panic has seized the country. . . . The issue is one which it is very painful for me to meet. On the one hand is the long night of oppression which will follow the return of our people to the 'Union'; on the other, the suffering of the women and children, and carnage among the few brave patriots who would still oppose the invader."[113] The armies of both sides were at that point essentially in a hold position, awaiting further instructions. Desertions continued among the Confederates. Capt. W. E. Stoney of Hagood's brigade of South Carolinians recorded in his diary on April 23 that twenty-two men from his unit left for home over a period of two days. "The division is being rapidly reduced in this way," he wrote, "they are going in large bodies and at all hours without an effort being made to stop them."[114]

General Sherman on April 23 received from Major Hitchcock a telegraph message indicating that he had returned from Washington to Morehead City and that he would travel to Raleigh overnight.[115] A report filed by A. M. Van Dyke, assistant adjutant general, with Gen. John A. Logan on April 23 indicates that the Union army was taking measures to arrest some of of the "bummers." At the same time, the officer acknowledged that enlisted men were committing many of the outrages. He wrote: "Lieutenant Freeman, aide-de-camp from these head-quarters, who went out to Franklinton Depot with a patrol, reports from there that the 'bummers' are dispersing and making their way to Raleigh. The general thinks that if your patrols are posted along this side of the river that many of them may be arrested. Lieutenant Freeman also reports that many of the outrages have been committed by men belonging to authorized foraging parties."[116]

April 24 (Monday)

At six o'clock in the morning Major Hitchcock returned to the Union head-quarters in Raleigh and, to Sherman's surprise, was accompanied by Gen. Ulysses S. Grant. Sherman wrote in his *Memoirs*: "I was both surprised and pleased to see the general [and] soon learned that my terms with Johnston had been disapproved." Grant instructed Sherman to give the forty-eight hours' notice required by the terms of the truce and afterward to proceed to resume hostilities if there were no surrender.[117]

Sherman was incensed by the disapproval and further outraged by the press coverage, particularly in the New York newspapers. One paper reported that Sherman had violated an agreement with Lincoln to accept nothing but surrender and not to negotiate. Sherman argued vehemently that there had been no such agreement. He directed his vitriol against Secretary of War Edwin Stanton, who, he believed, was behind the press charges.

Word of the truce suspension soon passed to Confederate headquarters. "I am instructed to limit my operations to your immediate command, and not to attempt civil negotiations," Sherman wrote to Johnston. "I therefore demand the surrender of your army on the same terms as were given to General Lee at Ap-pomattox, April 9th instant, purely and simply." Ironically, the notification came only one hour after official word arrived from Charlotte that Jefferson Davis had approved the terms as negotiated on April 17 and 18 at the Bennitt farmhouse.[118]

In letters to Governor Vance on April 24, General Johnston promised to do all within his powers to return to North Carolina items due the state from the Confederate government. He wrote: "[G]reat outrages are committed on your people by Confederate soldiers, I know, but they are the disbanded men of the army of Northn. Va. I regret this as much as you do, but can not, with my little force, prevent it. Indeed this army has probably suffered as much pro-portionally, as the people of the State. For crowds of these disbanded soldiers seize our subsistence stores whereever they find them."[119]

April 25 (Tuesday)

Sherman arranged a meeting with Johnston to renew negotiations at the Bennitt farmhouse the following day. In a formal communication to General Grant composed on April 25, Sherman defended his earlier terms. "I have not the least liking to interfere in the civil policy of our Government, but would shun it as something not to my liking," Sherman wrote. Without a negotiated peace, Sherman foresaw that "the rebel armies will disperse; and, instead of dealing with six or seven States, we will have to deal with numberless bands of desperadoes, headed by such men as Mosby, Forrest, Red Jackson, and others, who know not and care not for danger and its consequences."[120]

Two histories of Union regiments offer contrasting versions of the extent of foraging activities as of April 25. The Third Wisconsin Regiment led a march southwest from Raleigh to Holly Springs on that date. The officers instructed the men to "forage liberally on the country" during the thirteen-mile march.[121] James C. Rogers, a colonel with the 123d New York Regiment, recorded that on April 25 his outfit moved to Jones's Crossroads, where it remained for three days. "The entire march was without noticeable incident," wrote Rogers, continuing, "I desire, however, to speak of the good conduct of the men, who abstained without exception from the unsoldierly vice of straggling, and who uniformly treated the inhabitants of the country with kindness, and respected their property."[122] Rogers's report was part of an official record filed contemporaneously with the march and did not reflect his musings years later. His readiness to defend the activities of his men was typical of Union officers and betrayed a defensiveness about the public image of Sherman's army.

April 26 (Wednesday)

On the day that Sherman and Johnston reopened negotiations at the Bennitt farmhouse and formally ended the conflict for their armies, the Confederate cabinet met with Pres. Jefferson Davis at Charlotte and agreed to leave that same day with the aim of getting west of the Mississippi River. Attorney General George Davis of North Carolina parted company with the party at that point.[123]

The meeting at Mr. Bennitt's house commenced, as had the first, at noon. Johnston wrote that the two men, "anxious to prevent further bloodshed," agreed without difficulty on terms, using as their model the framework established by Grant and Lee at Appomattox. The Confederates were to deposit arms and property at Greensboro. Troops were to be given their parole upon pledging not to take up arms again. Side arms of officers and their private horses and baggage could be retained. All officers and men were permitted to return to their homes. Field transportation was to be loaned to the troops to help them get home, as well as for later use. A small quantity of arms would be retained and then deposited in state capitals. Troops from Texas and Arkansas were to be furnished water transportation. Surrender of naval forces within the limits of Johnston's command was also included.[124]

That evening, in Raleigh, General Grant approved the terms. Taking the original copy with him, he departed for Washington by way of New Bern. Sherman set into motion the details necessary to put the terms into effect, assigning to Gen. John M. Schofield the task of granting paroles and making out muster rolls and inventories of property for Johnston's army "at and about" Greensboro.[125] Gen. Jacob D. Cox, in his memoirs published in 1882, found in Sherman's willingness to adapt to circumstances evidence of the true soldier. He wrote:

> No trait of Sherman's character was more marked than his loyal subordination to his superiors in army rank or in the State. Full of confidence in his own views, and vigorous in urging them, he never complained at being overruled, and instantly adapted his military conduct to the orders he received when once debate was closed by specific directions from those in authority. He had shown this in the Vicksburg campaign and at Savannah; and, hurt and humiliated as he now was, his conduct as an officer was the same, though he resented the personal wrong. . . .[126]

The announcement of a peace settlement stirred another round of rejoicing among the Union soldiers, akin to if not surpassing that which met the initial news of peace. John C. Arbuckle of the Fourth Iowa Infantry recalled:

> When on the evening of April 26, 1865, we were officially notified that terms of surrender had been agreed upon and signed; the whole army went wild with rejoicing; flags and banners were all unfurled; the drum corps were called out; guns were fired; bonfires were kindled; we paraded the camp; gathered at the various headquarters of the commanding Generals and were entertained with thrilling and eloquent speeches. . . . It was a night never to be forgotten; not until the small hours of the morning did we lie down to dreams and sweet sleep.[127]

The scene in Raleigh was repeated in Greensboro, where the Federals on April 26 began processing the paroles, a task that would take until May 1. Confederate general William J. Hardee met Union general Schofield and a small detachment of the Twenty-third Corps on the rail line near Hillsborough and conducted them to Johnston's headquarters in a grove on the edge of Greensboro.[128]

Letitia Morehead Walker lived at Blandwood, perhaps the finest home in Greensboro. She later recalled the entry of the Union troops into the city:

> One fine morning, amid the sound of bugles and trumpets and bands of music, the Federals entered Greensboro, fully thirty thousand strong, to occupy the town for some time. General Cox was in command. He, [Gen. Ambrose E.] Burnside, Schofield, and General Kilpatrick, with their staffs, sent word to the Mayor that they would occupy the largest house in town that night, and until their headquarters were established. They came to Blandwood, which already sheltered three families and several sick soldiers. My father received them courteously and received them as guests—an act which General Cox appreciated. . . .
>
> These troops remained several (months) encamped on the hills around the town, and at sunset each evening the practicing of the various bands of music would again open the floodgates of tears. But with the morning sun the avaricious desire for their "greenbacks" seized the ladies of the town; chicken and fruit pies, beaten biscuits, ice cream, and cake poured through the camps. One company sent me a message that "the ice cream was not rich enough—needed more eggs." A few drops of tumeric (often used for yellow pickles) covered the difficulty and gave satisfaction.[129]

The scene and the welcome, needless to say, were far different from that offered to Union troops two weeks earlier in Raleigh. Ethel Stephens Arnett, who has written extensively about Greensboro, states that "it is a matter of record that during their occupation of Greensboro the officers of the Union showed the utmost consideration for owners of all homes occupied by their forces." Mrs. Jacob Smith of Greensboro counted the city as fortunate for the fact that guards were furnished to each family on request—"and indispensable they were whenever spring onions dared to lift their heads!"[130]

During the five days occupied by the granting of paroles in Greensboro, Confederate officers voiced mounting concern about widespread desertion in their ranks. Greensboro citizens were distressed at the condition of those Confederate soldiers who remained. "Many were hungry to the point of starvation, many were ragged and shoeless; but what was worse still to the fastidious minded," according to Mrs. Arnett, "was the fact that many were covered with lice and seven-year itch."[131]

The daunting task of issuing paroles for the thirty thousand Confederates was matched or exceeded by the inventory of arms. Despite the fact that this was a worn and beaten army, much in the way of ordnance remained. Union captain T. G. Baylor provided headquarters with a partial accounting of the bounty. Some of the items listed were: fifteen 12-pounder brass guns (howitzers), sixty-eight 12-pounder guns (brass), 2,342 Springfield rifle muskets, 341,500 rounds of elongated ball cartridges, and 980 sets of harness and traces. Other supplies, in lesser quantity, were received at Charlotte, Salisbury, Jamestown, and Hillsborough.[132]

Union captain George Pepper provided another perspective on the paroles of Confederates at Greensboro. After accounting for artillery pieces, Pepper commented on the fact that while horses were in short supply, such was not the case with horse thieves. He wrote:

We obtained 108 pieces of artillery, which were parked near the town, with limber-chests, caissons, and running gear, but little or no ammunition and no horses or mules, or wagons. All these were needed by the paroled army to carry their rations, private property, etc.

All the valuable horses were, of course, the "private property" of somebody, and were appropriated. Such was the scramble for horses and mules, that the officers had to keep a strict watch over their horses to prevent them from being stolen, but many lost their animals notwithstanding every precaution. Every horse or mule that could carry a man or any other burden had been gobbled.[133]

Ethel Stephens Arnett wrote that "a great rush was made by many of the demoralized and desperate men for horses and mules to carry them on their way, and nearly every citizen stood guard over his stables day and night."[134]

On the evening of April 26, around a campfire, Confederate officer Bromfield L. Ridley recorded his thoughts regarding surrender and the lost cause. He imagined how his former opponents might have felt at that same moment:

To-day we received the order to surrender, and now we are prisoners of war. We will start for our homes in a day or two, just as soon as our paroles can be made out.

And now around the camp fires tonight we are discussing the surrender. All is confusion and unrest, and the stern realization that we are subdued, and ruined, is upon us. The proud spirited Southern people, all in a state of the veriest, the most sublimated sorrow. Oh! how is it in the Yankee camp to-night? Rejoicing, triumphing and revelling in the idea of glory. Think of it, the big dog has simply got the little dog down. Two million and seven hundred thousand have gotten the upper hand of six hundred thousand, who have worn themselves weary after losing half—the giant has put his foot on the Lilliputian and calls it glory! Bosh![135]

The diary of Confederate captain W. E. Stoney offers a picture of a demoralized force, one in nearly complete disarray, openly participating in depredations. Stoney placed the blame for the lack of discipline squarely on the Confederate commanders. When Stoney recorded the following observations on April 26, his unit had that day marched ten miles on the Trinity College road southwest of Greensboro. He wrote:

May I ever be spared such a sight as I witnessed when the order to move was given. Whole regiments remained on the ground, refusing to obey. In the last ten days desertion had reduced [Brig. Gen. William W.] Kirkland's reserves from 1,600 to 300 men; [Gen. Thomas] Clingman's and the brigade of junior reserves from the same cause were each no stronger; Hagood's and [Brig. Gen. Alfred H.] Colquitt's brigades had suffered, but not so much. Now not more than forty men in each brigade followed Kirkland and Clingman on the ground. Officers as high as colonels, not only countenanced, but participated in the shameful conduct. Major Holland, of the North Carolina troops, formerly attached to our brigade, went off with all his men, and officers of higher rank did the same. . . . For all this demoralization I hold our higher officers responsible. All the sensational reports which have so loosened the bands of discipline originate at their headquarters, and many of them are playing first hands in the shameless appropriation of public property that is going on. This last remark applies principally to General Hardee's headquarters, and much feeling is elicited among the troops by the appropriation there of supplies intended and much needed by them.[136]

April 27 (Thursday)

On April 27, the day General Grant left Raleigh to return to Washington by way of Morehead City, plans were set for the march of Sherman's troops out of North Carolina to the capital city by way of Petersburg and Richmond. Sherman, in his Field Order No. 66, on April 27 set commands and routes for the armies departing the state. Gen. O. O. Howard would lead the Army of the Tennessee by way of Louisburg and Warrenton or points to the east of that line. Gen. Henry W. Slocum would lead the Army of Georgia into Virginia by way of Oxford. The Tenth Corps, under the command of Gen. Alfred H. Terry, and the Twenty-third Corps, led by Gen. John M. Schofield, would remain in North Carolina as garrison forces through the summer.[137] Sherman himself returned to Savannah and sailed from that port city to Washington.

Union assistant adjutant general A. M. Van Dyke, acting under orders from Gen. O. O. Howard, described the line of march for his forces. The Fifteenth Corps, commanded by Gen. John A. Logan, would follow the Louisburg road (present-day U.S. Highway 401), moving by way of Shocco Springs northward to Warrenton. The Seventeenth Corps, commanded by Gen. Frank P. Blair Jr., was assigned a route just east of the Raleigh and Gaston rail line by way of Jones's Spring, Warrenton, and Macon, crossing the Roanoke River near the mouth of Six-Pound Creek. The Twentieth Corps and the Fourteenth Corps, led by Gen. Alpheus S. Williams and Gen. Jefferson C. Davis respectively, would march on a more westerly route through Oxford. The march would commence on the morning of Saturday, April 29. Appended to the instructions concerning the lines of march were the following special orders pertaining to foraging and destruction:

> First. All foraging will cease. Corps commanders will obtain what supplies they may need in addition to those carried with them by sending their quartermaster and commissary in advance, who are required to purchase, paying the cash or giving proper vouchers. . . .
>
> Second. The provost guards will be selected with the greatest care and sent well ahead, so that every house may be guarded, and every possible precaution will be taken to prevent the misconduct of any straggler or marauder. Punishments for entering or pillaging houses will be severe and immediate. . . .[138]

The instructions to stop foraging marked a departure for the Union command, the first time in weeks that its troops did not have authority to rely on appropriated bounty for subsistence. M. Rochester, another Union assistant adjutant general, further detailed instructions regarding the end to foraging. He began with the following recommendations concerning the pace of the march, an issue that in the coming days became a point of contention both with officers and enlisted men:

> The march should be conducted in such a manner as to fatigue the troops as little as possible, the divisions being allowed, when practicable, to camp from three to five miles apart. It is expected that the troops will march about fifteen miles per day. No necessity will exist on this march for foraging, as the supplies taken in the wagons will be sufficient for us until we reach Richmond. No soldier will be allowed, on any pretense whatever, to enter a dwelling-house. Any found guilty of commiting robbery or any outrage upon citizens must be severely and summarily punished. Hostilities having ceased, every effort should be made to prevent lawless and dishonest men from bringing disgrace upon us, as we are about to return to our homes. No good soldier will refrain from aiding in the detection of all marauders and thieves. If forage or fresh beef is purchased on the march[,] payment should be made at time of purchase.[139]

Whereas the Union troops were well stocked with supplies for their march home, such was not the case with the Confederates in and around Greensboro. Johnston, in his negotiations with Sherman, had assumed that his own depots were adequately stocked. A few days before they marched, however, he learned of the extent of the raids. A fellow officer, Johnston wrote, "informed me that those depots had all been plundered by the crowd of fugitives and country-people, who thought, apparently, that, as there was no longer a government, they might assume the division of this property." Similar thefts of supplies had taken place in Charlotte. As a result, Johnston was left with little beyond a stock of cotton yarn and a small quantity of cloth. "[T]his was entirely inadequate; and great suffering would have ensued," he concluded. He turned to Sherman for help, and, informed of the Confederates' plight, the Union general supplied 250,000 rations. No conditions were placed on the gift—only the requirement that

Johnston arrange the transfer by rail from Morehead City. "This averted any danger of suffering or even inconvenience," Johnston asserted.[140] The generosity of the act likely also explained in part the warm relationship that developed between the two men in the postwar years.

April 28 (Friday)

On April 28, as he prepared to leave Raleigh for Savannah, Sherman summoned the corps commanders to his headquarters, where they reviewed future plans. In a written communication prepared for Grant on this date, Sherman looked to the future and anticipated problems to come with the South's reconstruction:

> We should not drive a people into anarchy, and it is simply impossible for our military power to reach all the masses of their unhappy country.
>
> I confess I did not desire to drive General Johnston's army into bands of armed men, going about without purpose, and capable only of infinite mischief. . . . I envy not the task of "reconstruction," and am delighted that the Secretary of War has relieved me of it.[141]

The last comment, of course, was directed toward Edwin Stanton, whom Sherman blamed for the criticism that he received following the initial negotiations at the Bennitt farmhouse.

All was in readiness for the march of the Union armies homeward. Maj. George Ward Nichols set the scene and offered thumbnail sketches of each of the corps:

> The orders are issued for the return of the army home. The 23d and 10th Corps, with Kilpatrick's gallant troopers, remain here to garrison the country. The rest—the faithful, patient 14th; the swift, tireless, heroic 15th; the tried veterans of the 17th; the noble, war-torn heroes of the 20th—companions of many a wearisome march and hasty bivouac— comrades upon many a battlefield—never defeated, always victorious, brothers always—are going to their homes, to be welcomed by the loving embrace of wife, mother, and sister— to meet the warm grasp of a brother's hand—to receive from the Nation the high honors she gladly and proudly pays to her gallant defenders.[142]

"We set our faces homeward," wrote Gen. William Hazen on April 28, "with feelings of thankfulness and joy no language can express."[143]

The march out of North Carolina and into Virginia, though rapid and almost forced, was nonetheless carefully regulated and well directed. Instructions prohibiting foraging had been distributed the previous day. Fred H. Wilson, an acting assistant adjutant general, reiterated and expanded upon those instructions:

> During the march from Raleigh, N.C., to Washington, D.C., via Richmond, full rations of hard bread or flour, meat, coffee, and salt, and half rations of sugar will be issued to the troops. No foraging will be allowed excepting by permission from these headquarters, and everything taken must be paid for. The division headquarters will see to the collection of forage for all the authorized animals in the division, giving vouchers (written in ink) to all from whom corn or fodder is taken. The division commissary will see to the collection of bacon and beef for the command, giving vouchers for all taken, and being careful to leave an ample supply with the families. Private property of every description, horses, mules,

harnesses, wagons, etc., will be respected. Straggling will be severely punished, and brigade commanders will, by a system of roll-calls and otherwise, take every precaution to prevent this evil. The troops must be kept in ranks while on the march, nor will any enlisted man be permitted to leave the column without authority from his regimental commanders. All unauthorized men found away from the line of march within any house, yard, garden, or inclosure, except to obtain water, will be promptly arrested by the mounted patrol or safeguard and turned over to the rear guard for punishment, at the discretion of the general commanding. There will be an advance guard leading the division each day, whose duty shall be the establishing of safeguards over the dwellings and property along the route, preventing of all straggling toward the head of the column, and enforcement of these orders with the utmost vigor. There will also be a strong rear guard, the duty of which will be to keep the rear of the column constantly well closed up, to prevent straggling toward the rear, to promptly arrest any offender who may violate these orders, and to receive all prisoners that may be turned over by the division during the day. . . .[144]

Rumors circulated that Sherman's army would continue to forage and plunder. Catherine Edmondston of Halifax County, writing in her diary on April 28, based much of her entry on speculation, fear, and rumor. She objected to the plans to march the troops out of the state when they might have been transported by rail to the North Carolina coast and then shipped north, and she suspected Sherman of ulterior motives for the plan. She wrote:

The route that he proposes to follow lies thro' Oxford, Danville, & Lynchburg & then down the undevastated portion of Va (if he can find it!) to Alexandria. Says he will sweep a path of from 50 to 75 miles wide perfectly bare of *all* forage & will take such provisions & animals as he will need. Professes an unwillingness to rob the people & hypocritically whines over the suffering he must cause, but gives the lie to his scruples by not shipping his army from New Berne, Wilmington, & Petersburg, all ports within easy reach of him. It needs no seer to divine his object in his cruel & murderous act. It is to disable and cripple us so much the more & to make us dependant [*sic*] upon the North for our very existence. Would that the women & children who will be starved & die by his cruelty could haunt every moment sleeping or waking of his future life. He runs ten trains per day between Morehead City & Raleigh & sends out numbers of forage parties daily, three hundred waggons in a party, who forage the country for 50 miles to find food for his army.[145]

Indications are that foraging activities by the Union troops in the coming days were kept to a minimum. Accounts from Franklin and Warren Counties, through which the greatest number of soldiers marched, record that raids on smokehouses were the principal form of plunder. Theft of livestock, as compared with the rest of the march through North Carolina, was greatly reduced if not eliminated.

Meanwhile Confederate troops, short on supplies to start, made their way through the Piedmont as best they could. Bromfield L. Ridley recorded in his diary on April 28 that he and a fellow officer with the Army of Tennessee "concluded to get ahead of the disbanded army on the way home, so we could forage for man and beast."[146] Capt. W. E. Stoney on April 28 received his parole and last pay, a dollar and a quarter in silver. He judged it to be part of the last of the Confederate treasury and declared it his intention to "have mine made into a medal to keep and value as received from the dying hands of my government."[147]

April 29 (Saturday)

On April 29 the greater part of Sherman's army began the march north. Sherman himself departed by rail this day for Wilmington and traveled from there to Savannah, which he reached on May 1.[148] The Seventeenth Corps marched from Raleigh toward Forestville, a community just south of present-day Wake Forest. The Fifteenth Corps took a more northeasterly route out of Raleigh, crossing the Neuse River at Rogers Crossroads (later known as Wake Crossroads).[149]

Officers placed bets on whose men could march the fastest to Richmond and, in some cases, drove their troops as far as thirty-five miles per day in the May heat and humidity of North Carolina and Virginia. Consequently, many fell ill or lagged behind. According to historian Joseph T. Glatthaar, "dozens who had survived the war died of heat prostration." The bets and the forced march were, in many cases, the responsibility of junior officers left in charge by the corps commanders in Sherman's absence. Their decisions enraged the troops. "This brutality should be investigated," a lieutenant in the Army of the Tennessee complained. According to a sergeant in the Army of Georgia, "We have never made a much harder march and some of our Generals deserve to have their necks broke for such 'Tom foolery' after the war."[150]

A veteran of the march, a member of the Fifty-fifth Illinois Regiment, recalled years later:

The result of this amicable race was a disorganized and fagged-out column of troops put to the severest test of endurance. Brigades would be ordered to take the road in the middle of the night in order to steal around other troops and get in the advance. There was more straggling and actual suffering from fatigue in this march, perhaps, than in any other during the Carolina campaign. Thirty-five miles a day were made by some commands. The first warm weather of the season had come, making the tramp doubly exhausting to the men, and several fatal sun-strokes were reported.[151]

Charles W. Wills, also from Illinois, commented on the pace of the march, the heat, and the conduct of his men:

Left Raleigh at 7 this morning on my way home, via Richmond and Washington. Made about 11 miles. Rather too warm for such fast marching as we always do. If we could just make 15 miles a day, say 10 of it between sunrise and 10 a.m., and the remainder after 2 p.m., it would not hurt a man or an animal, but we move when we do move at three or three and a half miles an hour, and not all even Sherman's men can stand it in as warm weather as this. I saw a number laid out this morning by the roadside looking as if they had been boiled. The 50 pounds of equipment is what uses them up. Well settled country, and it looks beautiful. . . .

We are on our good behavior this trip. No foraging, no bumming rails, or houses, and nothing naughty whatever. We have the best set of men in the world. When it is in order to raise h--- they have no equals in destructiveness and ability to hate and worry, or superiors as to fighting Rebels, but now they have none, and they are perfect lambs. Not a hand laid on a rail this evening with intent to burn, not a motion toward a chicken or smoke-house, not a thing in their actions that even a Havelock would object to. They don't pretend to love our "erring brethren" yet, but no conquered foe could ask kinder treatment than all our men seem disposed to give these Rebels. . . .[152]

Wills's comments were typical of those of Union officers about their men. Defensive about their conduct, they were quick to draw a contrast between their actions on the earlier part of the march and their demeanor after the peace negotiations.

Other Union soldiers had more pleasant memories of the resumption of the march. A member of the Fifty-third Ohio Volunteer Infantry Regiment who crossed the Neuse River on April 29 reported that his outfit passed "through a poor section of North Carolina" but that the "weather was delightful."[153] Capt. George Pepper wrote that "the woods, in all their wealth of tint and color, shaken with the softest breezes, as with a bannered panoply, attend our march," adding, "the music of the bands precedes us, ringing through the gorges and passes of the hills."[154] A history of the Third Wisconsin Regiment refers to the post-Raleigh segment of the route as "the most joyous march of its service."[155]

Anna Fuller of Louisburg, who had been dreading the arrival of the Union troops for weeks, on April 29 received definite word of their approach. She wrote in her diary:

> A squad of Yankee cavalry entered town and stopped in front of our house. They came to tell of the approach of the Army, a large portion of which will pass through here Monday and Tuesday. . . . We have lived in constant dread of them for the last two weeks. . . . A guard [was] appointed to protect the town from the "Bummers," a set of lawless men who come before and follow after the Army, to plunder and destroy everything in their way. . . . Some Negroes [have] gone to the Yankees, then only to return asking pardon of [their] masters.[156]

Less well documented is the march homeward of Confederate troops at this point in time. Bromfield L. Ridley reported on April 29 from near Lexington that "a great many people visited us to exchange forage for spun thread; that is our currency now."[157] His statement substantiates General Johnston's earlier indication that cloth was among the few items in ready supply in the Confederate stores.

April 30 (Sunday)

Those regiments in Sherman's army that had not taken up the march on Saturday, April 29, did so the following day. (The exceptions were the troops of the Tenth and Twenty-third Corps, who would remain in North Carolina until later in the summer.) In expectation of their arrival, fifty bakers traveled from Baltimore, Philadelphia, and New York to Washington to assist with rations for the planned Grand Review of the army.[158] Gen. Jacob D. Cox wrote that the men in gray "took up the journey homeward—to many of them a long and weary one—to begin anew the struggle of life in an almost universal impoverishment." Cox recalled how the Union "columns marched northward with flying colors and swell of martial music, full of hope and enthusiasm, to take part in the memorable review at Washington."[159]

On Sunday morning Gen. O. O. Howard, "true to his Christian instincts," ordered the Fifteenth and Seventeenth Corps to observe the Sabbath. "To us, the weary and way worn, how great was the joy!'' wrote a member of the Fifty-third Ohio Regiment.[160] The Third Wisconsin Regiment was among the units taking up the march on April 30. According to its regimental history, spirits were high:

[T]he bands playing "Home again," and "We are homeward bound," and the troops in the most joyous spirits. In nine days Richmond was reached—170 miles, an average of nearly nineteen miles a day. On the way people thronged on the roadside to see the army pass. All pronounced themselves glad the war was over; and the kindliest feeling was expressed. Every night some of Lee's men, on their homeward journey, came into camp; and were fed most generously by the Union soldiers, who in fact lived on half-rations, because they made so liberal contribution from their haversacks to the many visiting Confederates to feed them and give them a few meals on their journey. The forager's occupation was now gone. Not a "bummer" left the ranks, not a house or field was invaded, nor goose or chicken disturbed.[161]

Cornelia Phillips Spencer also wrote about the encounters between Union and Confederate soldiers. Bitter enemies only days earlier, members of the two armies found common ground and broke bread together. Mrs. Spencer wrote:

But I am glad to say that wherever a Federal soldier met any of them [Confederate soldiers], he was prompt to offer help and food, and express a kindly and soldierly cordiality. Grant's men, they all said, had been especially generous. There was something worth studying in the air and expression of these men, a something which had a beneficial and soothing effect on the observers. They were not unduly cast down, nor had any appearance of the humiliation that was burning into our souls. They were serious, calm, and self-possessed. They said they were satisfied that all had been done that could be done. . . .[162]

Rice C. Bull of the 123d New York Infantry, which remained in Raleigh until April 30, recounted his view of the march:

[W]e began the "Homeward March" from Raleigh, North Carolina, the last, and to me, I can truly say, the happiest made by Sherman's army. It was to differ greatly from any made by us that preceded it. As in our other marches we were to carry our usual load of goods and equipment but our cartridge boxes were emptied of all but five cartridges. We were to go through the country from Raleigh to Washington in an orderly manner, no straggling would be allowed; there were to be no foragers to gather food from the area through which we passed and no destruction of property of any kind would be permitted.

The New Yorker's opinion of the landscape differed from those of most of his compatriots. He stated that the "country from Raleigh to Richmond did not appeal strongly to us northern people." The countryside, he later recalled, was "mostly wooded, and where farms were cultivated, they did not look prosperous." Nearly all buildings, he found, were "poor and ill-kept."[163]

May 1 (Monday)

The beginning of a new month was marked by the entry of the Fifteenth and Seventeenth Corps of Sherman's army into Franklin County and its seat at Louisburg. Numerous accounts left by Union soldiers and local residents illustrate the seismic effect of thousands of troops on the community, to that date untouched directly by the war. Scores of local families had contributed their sons to the Confederate cause, of course, but the presence of an occupying army was altogether a different element with which to contend.

Union general William Hazen recorded the progress of his men on May 1. Beginning at six o'clock in the morning from just south of Rolesville in Wake County, they marched eighteen miles, crossing the Little River, Crooked Creek, and Cedar Creek, and camped for the evening on the south side of the Tar River just across from the town of Louisburg. George P. Metz, a Union soldier, offered a similar account, observing, "Oh what a difference—nothing is destroyed—everything is protected—no fences burned."[164] In his diary, Charles Brown Tompkins described Louisburg as "the prettiest little place I ever saw" and observed that the town's "Negroes shouted and acted as though they were crazy."[165]

Anna Fuller expressed in her diary her surprise that the Union soldiers to that point had been well behaved. Like Tompkins, she commented on the reaction of the town's blacks to the arrival of the Union army:

> I am bewildered and my head is sick. The town is full of soldiers, riding and walking up and down every street and coming into our yards and kitchens. This morning the cavalry entered about ten o'clock *and have been coming all day.* I must say for them, they have behaved very orderly, so far. Their tents are pitched in the College and Male Academy groves. . . . Would that I could describe my feelings, but I have not the power. The reality is upon us, that we are a subjugated people. . . . The Negroes seem wild with excitement; they expect now to be free, and never more do any work, but poor deluded creatures, they are sadly mistaken.[166]

A member of the Fifty-fifth Illinois Regiment wrote that "the people, white and black, all along the route greeted us with demonstrations of joy."[167]

Among former slaves interviewed by field workers for the Federal Writers' Project of the WPA in the 1930s was Mary Anderson of Raleigh, who in 1865 was fourteen years old and lived with her family on the plantation of Sam Brodie southeast of Mapleville in Franklin County. Brodie's plantation house no longer stands but was located just off Ferrell's Bridge Road. It stood on the eastern-flanking line of march taken by the Fifteenth Corps of Sherman's army. Anderson's account offers insight into the reactions both of masters and slaves to the arrival of the emancipators:

> The plantation was very large, and there were about two hundred acres of cleared land that was farmed each year. . . .
> There were about 162 slaves on the plantation. . . .
> The war was begun, and there were stories of fights and freedom. The news went from plantation to plantation, and while the slaves acted natural and some even more polite than usual, they prayed for freedom.
> Then one day I heard something that sounded like thunder, and Missus and Marster were whispering to each other. The grown slaves were whispering to each other. Sometimes they gathered in little gangs in the grove. Next day I heard it again, boom, boom, boom. I went and asked Missus, "Is it going to rain?" She said, "Mary, go to the icehouse and bring me some pickles and preserves." I went and got them. She ate a little and gave me some. Then she said, "You run along and play." In a day or two, everybody on the plantation seemed to be disturbed, and Marster and Missus were crying. Marster ordered all the slaves

to come to the great house at nine o'clock. Nobody was working, and slaves were walking over the grove in every direction.

At nine o'clock, all the slaves gathered at the great house, and Marster and Missus come out on the porch and stood side by side. You could hear a pin drop, everything was so quiet. Then Marster said "Good morning," and Missus said, "Good morning, children." They were both crying. Then Marster said, "Men, women, and children, you are free. You are no longer my slaves. The Yankees will soon be here."

Marster and Missus then went into the house, got two large armchairs, put them on the porch facing the avenue, and sat down side by side and remained there watching. In about an hour, there was one of the blackest clouds coming up the avenue from the main road. It was the Yankee soldiers. They finally filled the mile-long avenue from Marster's house to the main Louisburg Road and spread out over the mile-square grove.

The mounted men dismounted. The footmen stacked their shining guns and began to build fires and cook. They called the slaves, saying, "You are free." Slaves were whooping and laughing and acting like they were crazy. Yankee soldiers were shaking hands with the Negroes and calling them Sam, Dinah, Sarah, and asking them questions. They busted the door to the smokehouse and got all the hams. They went to the icehouse and got several barrels of brandy, and such a time. The Negroes and Yankees were cooking and eating together. The Yankees told them to come on and join them, they were free.

Marster and Missus sat on the porch, and they were so humble no Yankee bothered anything in the great house. The slaves were awfully excited. The Yankees stayed there, cooked, ate, drank, and played music until about night. Then a bugle began to blow and you never saw such getting on horses and lining up in your life. In a few minutes they began to march, leaving the grove, which was soon as silent as a graveyard. They took Marster's horses and cattle with them and joined the main army and camped just across Cypress Creek one and one-half miles from my Marster's place on the Louisburg Road.[168]

Mary Anderson's view of the events of 1865 is valuable on several counts. First, of course, is the fact that the perspective is that of an African American, a former slave who stood to gain her freedom as a consequence. Second, the testimony contradicts the contention that no foraging went on once the troops were north of Raleigh. Anderson specifically mentions the raiding of the smokehouses, the consumption of brandy, and the theft of horses from the plantation.

Nevertheless, the contrast between the behavior of the soldiers on this portion of the march and the men's earlier conduct was striking to most Union observers. Charles W. Wills was an Illinois officer. He wrote: "It seems like the early days of my soldiering to see the citizens all at home, their horses and mules in the stables, and gardens full of vegetables passed untouched. When a man can pass an onion bed without going for them, and they did a number of them today, no one need talk to me of total depravity."[169]

Years later, Robert W. Winston, member of a prominent North Carolina family, judge, and writer, offered another perspective on the arrival of the Yankees in Franklin County. In his autobiography, *It's a Far Cry*, published in 1937, Winston recalled that in May 1865, at the age of five, he sat on a set of steps beside his home alongside Lundsay, a black boy about his same age. The scene he witnessed remained vivid sixty years later:

For several days we had been expecting the triumphant Union troops to march through Springfield, our refugee plantation, on their way north. Expectation was at tip-toe. Ever since Sherman's easy victory over Johnston, at the last pitched battle of the war, known as Bentonville, the wildest rumors had been afloat. The grapevine telegraph told of a mighty Yankee host, in bright uniforms, with brass buttons and pockets bulging with real money. Finally the eventful day had arrived. In the distance, Lundsay and I could catch the rub-a-dub-dub of the kettledrum and the notes of the fife.

Nearer came the sound of marching feet and soon our ten-acre grove was alive with Blue Coats. Almost in a moment horses were unhitched and fed, tents, white and circus-like, arose and a little city sprang up. Soldiers by the hundreds began to wander through the slave quarters and around our dwelling. But neither Lundsay nor I seemed to be alarmed, we were much too young and too busy with the sight of huge caissons and muskets with bayonets fixed, and knapsacks and canteens and jolly, rollicking soldiers wearing the queerest looking flat-topped caps, whose brims stretched far out to the front.

The following day the troops marched on their way without having damaged the property. Winston reckoned that the reason they were spared was that his father, Patrick Henry Winston, had attended the University of North Carolina with the commander of the division, Gen. Frank P. Blair Jr.[170] The Winstons had refugeed inland from their home in Bertie County to avoid the effects of the war. Their Franklin County home, which was on the western-flanking line of march for the Fifteenth Corps, still stands northeast of Franklinton near Mitchiners Crossroads.

Many of the troops camped on the grounds of Louisburg College. E. H. Davis, Franklin County historian, was the son of the college president. Born in 1860, Davis, like Mary Anderson and Robert W. Winston, had childhood memories of the arrival of the Union troops. Davis remembered distinctly the face of Gen. John A. Logan. At the age of five, Davis accompanied his father to the school grounds, where the commotion produced by the incoming troops had disrupted classes. "The whole grove—the town as well—was full of blue coats," he recalled. He remembered the rows upon rows of tents. The old academy building had been filled to the point of bursting with corn brought in from outlying areas to feed horses belonging to Union cavalrymen. Despite the numbers, Davis contended, the few days of occupation were attended "with no violent disorder of any sort."[171]

Elsewhere in the state Bromfield L. Ridley continued his march homeward with other Confederate soldiers. On May 1 he reported that forage was "scarce." Chores such as shoeing mules and repairing wagons occupied the soldiers' time. At the invitation of wealthy planter Peter Hairston, some of the officers partook of the hospitality at his elegant house at Cooleemee. "Stragglers made an effort to get our mules last night, but failed," Ridley wrote, "after a few shots from our Irish guards who are sleeping on this campaign with one eye open."[172]

May 2 (Tuesday)

Wave upon wave of Union soldiers continued to roll through Louisburg on May 2. Gen. William Hazen crossed the Tar River and passed through town at 8:30 A.M. By nightfall, after marching eighteen miles, his men were encamped near present-day Inez in Warren County. In conversation with area planters, Union captain George Pepper found them to be "honestly and earnestly in sympathy with the anti-slavery policy of the Administration," adding that "they deeply deplore the murder of the President."[173] William M. Davis of the Fourth Minnesota Volunteer Infantry Regiment, part of the Fifteenth Corps, also met several of the local residents. Like other Union diarists, he found the landscape inviting and the people, white as well as black, welcoming. He wrote:

Saw some beautiful plantations, well fenced, well cultivated, and I think must be very productive. The citizens are a much better class than those in South Carolina or southern North Carolina. They are much better dressed, more intelligent and more enterprising. Their dwellings are always neat and adorned with taste—often elegant—with splendid grounds adjacent. The country is superior in all respects to any that I have seen since leaving west Tennessee. There are many plantations which I would be content to own and reside upon. They have unmistakably the home air. Ladies, men and children thronged to the road sides to look at us and hear our bands play. Many of the whites are Union people. The Negroes are all loyal and often clap their hands and shout, "Bress de Lord! We's glad to see ye!" and like expressions of joy.[174]

Expressions of joy were far from the mind of Anna Fuller of Louisburg. On May 2 she recorded in her diary her strong feelings concerning the events of the past two days: "This morning a few cavalry companies came in, followed by bands of music and then the infantry, to number 12,000 to 15,000 men, then came the wagon train, which was very long. . . . [W]ithin my breast not a single emotion of patriotism or pleasure, I felt indignant. Our house was kept closed, while they were passing and so were the neighbors, as far as I could see."[175]

In Greensboro the mustering-out of Confederates, which had begun on April 26, concluded by May 2. Officers processed rosters, issued paroles, stacked arms, and divided rations, wagons, and horses among the parolees. A military chest containing thirty-nine thousand dollars arrived from Richmond, and each man received $1.29 for his journey home. In the words of D. Augustus Dickert, captain in a South Carolina brigade, "this remnant of a once grand army bent their steps toward their desolate homes." The men found it advisable to move by different routes, taking byways so as to avoid those Union regiments that remained.[176]

Gen. Joseph E. Johnston bade his men farewell and gave them their final instructions in his General Order No. 22, issued on May 2: "In terminating our official relations, I earnestly exhort you to observe faithfully the terms of pacification agreed upon; and to discharge the obligations of good and peaceful citizens, as well as you have performed the duties of thorough soldiers in the field."[177]

Writing in his *Narrative*, Johnston commended the occupying Union troops that remained in the South as garrisons after the peace. In doing so, he drew a contrast between those Northerners posted in the South on military duty and those with postwar political responsibilities:

The United States troops that remained in the Southern States, on *military* duty, conducted themselves as if they thought that the object of the war had been the restoration of the Union. They treated the people around them as they would have done those of Ohio or New York if stationed among them, as their fellow-citizens. Those people supposed, not unnaturally, that if those who had fought against them were friendly, the great body of the Northern people, who had not fought, must be more so. This idea inspired in them a kindlier feeling to the people of the North and the Government of the United States, than that existing ten years before. It created, too, a strong expectation that the Southern States would soon resume their places in the Union. The most despondent apprehended no such "reconstruction" as that subsequently established by Congress.[178]

May 3 (Wednesday)

On May 3 the central line of march and two flanking lines of the Fifteenth Corps reunited in southern Warren County and marched into the county seat at Warrenton. The Seventeenth Corps would reunite with the Fifteenth north of Warrenton, while the Fourteenth and Twentieth Corps would continue their line of march northward through Oxford and into Virginia at a point about thirty miles west of the town.[179]

Gen. William Hazen's day was typical. Beginning at eight o'clock in the morning, he and his men commenced their march, crossing Rich Neck and Fishing Creeks and passing through Warrenton at ten o'clock. They crossed the Raleigh and Gaston Railroad near Macon at one o'clock in the afternoon and camped that evening on the Roanoke River, having marched a total of twenty-four miles.[180] William M. Davis of the Fourth Minnesota Regiment followed the same course. "We marched today through woods, on cowpaths, and anyway to get along," he wrote on May 3, adding, "The country along the line of today's march [is] much the same as yesterday—rolling, with rich plantations, fine residences and good timber."[181]

The men of the Fifty-third Ohio Regiment were up at five o'clock in the morning and on the road an hour later. In Warrenton they encountered a group of former Confederate soldiers and exchanged pleasantries:

> A novel and inspiring sight greeted us as we were passing through this village. A squad of ex-Confederate officers stood by the wayside and reviewed us en route. If within a few short days these same officers had presented themselves to our view, our compliments and cards would have been tossed to them with a minie ball; but in lieu of such acts of legalized murder such interrogatories and remarks as these were made: "How are you, Johnnies?" "Are you glad you are alive?" "How do you enjoy peace?" "Did you find your wives and babies well?" "We are on the road to see our wives, babies, mothers, fathers, and sweethearts." "Say, Johnny, we abandoned a lot of lame mules at Raleigh, go and get them and go to farming." And much more of the same character. Here for the first time in months our eyes were greeted by the sight of refined womanhood. . . . To see these haggard veterans tip their hats in recognition of virtue and womanhood would have softened the hardest heart. . . .[182]

Capt. George Pepper described Warrenton as "a neat and picturesque village. . . . [I]t has a very attractive and imposing appearance." He wrote that he "longed for more time, so that I might feed on the enchantment for hours."[183] The rapid pace of the march precluded much interaction with the citizens of the town.

Nonetheless, Lizzie Montgomery, a Warrenton historian writing in 1924, indicated that several local people, some of whom had U.S. Army associations predating the conflict, entertained soldiers in their homes. "Of course," Mrs.

Montgomery wrote, "the majority had a very deep-seated hostility to the Federal government and all connected with it." Many of them, including the author's father, secured guards to watch over their property. In advance of the troops' arrival, her father, like others, had hidden his valuables. He carried his silver, watches, jewelry, and the like to the outlying farm of a Mr. Askew. As luck would have it, the Fifteenth Corps camped on the evening of May 3 on the banks of the Roanoke River on the same Mr. Askew's plantation. On the army's departure, members of the family recovered the box; the valuables were safe, but "they came perilously near getting the treasure." Approximately one hundred Union soldiers under a Captain Crapeau remained in Warrenton through the fall to keep order. They were lodged in the courthouse, according to Mrs. Montgomery.[184]

May 4 (Thursday)

May 4 was the day that Sherman's troops, or at least the greater part of them, marched out of North Carolina and into Virginia. Elsewhere in the state Governor Vance arrived in Statesville and rejoined his family.[185]

Relatively small detachments of garrison troops were posted in Warrenton, Louisburg, and other towns through the summer and into the fall. Diarist Anna Fuller of Louisburg remained filled with "dread and terror." She wrote on May 4: "Thinking all Yankees gone, another Regiment arrives to execute orders to free slaves and require owners to pay wages."[186]

Most Union soldiers who kept an account of the march made some reference to their departure from the Tar Heel State, following a stay of more than two months, and their passage into the Old Dominion. The Fifty-third Ohio Regiment, encamped with most of the others in the Fifteenth Corps, crossed the Roanoke River on a pontoon bridge. "Soon thereafter we crossed the state line of North Carolina into 'old Virginny,'" according to a regimental history.[187] When the Third Wisconsin Regiment reached the boundary, it found that a cracker box had been set up there with the words "State Line" written on it. The bands of the Twentieth Corps, of which that unit was a part, played "Carry Me Back to Ole Virginny."[188]

Capt. George Pepper journeyed from Warrenton to the Roanoke River on May 4. At the ferry where he crossed, Pepper noted, the river descended in a series of cascades and presented a "harmonious . . . combination of the beautiful in nature." Shortly thereafter he crossed the state line. Writing in reference to war-scarred Virginia, Pepper indicated that "the country in which Grant and Lee fought, presents to the eye *one vast sheet* of misery."[189]

Postscript

Several more days of marching through Virginia lay ahead for the men of Sherman's army. Within a week most had arrived in Washington, D.C., by way of Petersburg and Richmond. On May 23 and 24, the Fourteenth, Fifteenth, Seventeenth, and Twentieth Corps took part in the Grand Review of Union troops in the capital city. Gen. William T. Sherman sat on the reviewing platform on Pennsylvania Avenue alongside Gen. Ulysses S. Grant, Pres. Andrew Johnson, and members of the cabinet. As his men passed the stand, Sherman swelled with pride. He later wrote in his *Memoirs*:

> It was, in my judgment, the most magnificent army in existence—sixty-five thousand men, in splendid *physique*, who had just completed a march of nearly two thousand miles in a hostile country, in good drill, and who realized that they were being closely scrutinized by thousands of their fellow-countrymen and by foreigners. . . . Many good people, up to that time, had looked upon our Western army as a sort of mob; but the world then saw, and recognized the fact, that it was an army in the proper sense, well organized, well commanded and disciplined; and there was no wonder that it had swept through the South like a tornado. . . .[190]

Sherman's words of tribute to his men demonstrated at once his awareness of the reputation they had gained and his defensiveness about their conduct. The behavior of Sherman's men would continue to be the subject of debate for generations to come.

NOTES

1. Joseph E. Johnston, *Narrative of Military Operations Directed, During the late War Between the States* (originally published, 1874; Bloomington, Ind.: Indiana University Press, 1959; reprinted Millwood, N.Y.: Kraus, 1981), 396–399.

2. Johnson Hagood, *Memoirs of the War of Secession From the Original Manuscripts of Johnson Hagood* (Columbia: The State Company, 1910), 368.

3. Cornelia Phillips Spencer, *The Last Ninety Days of the War in North-Carolina* (New York: Watchman Publishing Company, 1866), 146.

4. J. G. de Roulhac Hamilton, ed., *The Correspondence of Jonathan Worth*, 2 vols. (Raleigh: North Carolina Historical Commission, 1909), 2:1288.

5. Katharine M. Jones, *When Sherman Came: Southern Women and the "Great March"* (Indianapolis: Bobbs-Merrill, 1964), 300.

6. Spencer, *Last Ninety Days*, 146.

7. William Tecumseh Sherman, *Memoirs of General W. T. Sherman* (originally published, 1886; reprint, New York: Library of America, 1990), 832.

8. Sherman, *Memoirs*, 832; John G. Barrett, *Sherman's March through the Carolinas* (Chapel Hill: University of North Carolina Press, 1956), 207.

9. K. Jack Bauer, ed., *Soldiering: The Civil War Diary of Rice C. Bull, 123rd New York Volunteer Infantry.* (San Rafael, Calif.: Presidio Press, 1977), 240.

10. John C. Arbuckle, *Civil War Experiences of a Foot-Soldier Who Marched with Sherman* (Columbus, Ohio: the author, 1930), 146.

11. George Ward Nichols, *The Story of the Great March* (New York: Harper and Brothers, 1865; Williamston, Mass: Corner House Publishers, 1972), 293.

12. W. Buck Yearns and John G. Barrett, eds., *North Carolina Civil War Documentary* (Chapel Hill: University of North Carolina Press, 1980), 337.

13. Barrett, *Sherman's March*, 211.

14. Barrett, *Sherman's March*, 210–215.

15. *The War of the Rebellion: A Compilation of the Official Records of the Union and Confederate Armies*, ser. 1, 47, pt. 3:172 (hereafter cited as *Official Records . . . Armies*).

16. *Official Records . . . Armies*, ser. 1, 47, pt. 3:188–189.

17. *Raleigh Daily Progress*, April 15, 1865.

18. Clara D. Maclean, "The Last Raid," *Southern Historical Society Papers* 13 (1885): 469–473.

19. Johnston, *Narrative*, 398–401, 417.

20. *The Story of the Fifty-fifth Illinois Volunteer Infantry in the Civil War, 1861–1865* (Clinton, Mass.: W. J. Coulter, 1887), 430.

21. *Raleigh Daily Progress*, April 15, 1865.

22. Spencer, *Last Ninety Days*, 157, 165–166.

23. *Raleigh Daily Progress*, April 15, 1865.

24. Barrett, *Sherman's March*, 218–219.

25. David L. Swain, *Early Times in Raleigh: Addresses Delivered by the Hon. David L. Swain, LL.D. at the Dedication of Tucker Hall* (Raleigh: Walters, Hughes and Company, 1867), 89; Spencer, *Last Ninety Days*, 160–161.

26. Spencer, *Last Ninety Days*, 160–161; Barrett, *Sherman's March*, 221.

27. Spencer, *Last Ninety Days*, 161–162.

28. Margaret Devereux, *Plantation Sketches* (Cambridge, Mass: Riverside Press, 1906), 150.

29. Edwin E. Bryant, *History of the Third Regiment of Wisconsin Veteran Volunteer Infantry, 1861–1865* (Cleveland: Arthur H. Clark Company, 1891), 329.

30. Bauer, *Soldiering*, 241.

31. Arbuckle, *Civil War Experiences*, 146–147.

32. *Story of the Fifty-fifth Illinois*, 430.

33. Jones, *When Sherman Came*, 300.

34. Elizabeth Reid Murray, *Wake: Capital County of North Carolina* (Raleigh: Capital County Publishing Company, 1983), 521.

35. Sherman, *Memoirs*, 834.

36. Spencer, *Last Ninety Days*, 173–174.

37. Spencer, *Last Ninety Days*, 174–175. On the life of Charles Manly, see *Dictionary of North Carolina Biography*, s.v. "Manly, Charles."

38. *Raleigh Daily Progress*, April 15, 1865.

39. Spencer, *Last Ninety Days*, 175–177.

40. Murray, *Wake*, 503, 514.

41. Devereux, *Plantation Sketches*, 156–157.

42. Devereux, *Plantation Sketches*, 159–163.

43. Jones, *When Sherman Came*, 307–308.

44. Barrett, *Sherman's March*, 249; Murray, *Wake*, 502; J. T. Trowbridge, *The South: A Tour of Its Battlefield and Ruined Cities, A Journey Through the Desolated States, and Talks with the People* (Hartford, Conn.: L. Stebbins, 1866), 581–582.

45. *Raleigh Daily News*, 1877, unknown date (item from scrapbook collection of William Richardson, Concord).

46. H. C. Olive, *The Life and Times of Rev. Johnson Olive* (Raleigh: Edwards and Broughton, 1886), 235–237, quoted in Murray, *Wake*, 526.

47. Henry Hitchcock, *Marching With Sherman: Passages from the Letters and Campaign Diaries of Henry Hitchcock*, ed. M. A. DeWolfe Howe (New Haven: Yale University Press, 1927), 297–298.

48. Thomas Ruffin to David L. Swain, August [?], 1865, Walter Clark Papers, Private Collections, State Archives, Division of Archives and History, Raleigh.

49. *Raleigh Daily News*, 1877, unknown date (item from scrapbook collection of William Richardson, Concord).

50. Robert E. Denney, *The Civil War Years: A Day-by-Day Chronicle of the Life of a Nation* (New York: Sterling Publishing Co., 1992), 559.

51. Spencer, *Last Ninety Days*, 213.

52. Barrett, *Sherman's March*, 223; James M. McPherson, *Battle Cry of Freedom: The Civil War Era* (New York: Oxford University Press, 1988), 830.

53. Hitchcock, *Marching With Sherman*, 298.

54. Sherman, *Memoirs*, 835.

55. Barrett, *Sherman's March*, 229.

56. William Carey Dodson and Joseph Wheeler, *Campaigns of Wheeler and His Cavalry, 1862–1865* (Atlanta: Hudgins Publishing Company, 1899), 357; Spencer, *Last Ninety Days*, 169.

57. Spencer, *Last Ninety Days,* 164.

58. Hitchcock, *Marching With Sherman*, 300.

59. Diary of Anna L. Fuller, April 15, 1865, Cecil W. Robbins Library, Louisburg College, Louisburg.

60. *Official Records . . . Armies*, ser. 1, 47, pt. 3:225.

61. *Official Records . . . Armies*, ser. 1, 47, pt. 3:225.

62. Hagood, *Memoirs of the War of Secession*, 368.

63. Sherman, *Memoirs*, 835; Johnston, *Narrative*, 401.

64. Ethel Stephens Arnett, *Confederate Guns Were Stacked, Greensboro, North Carolina* (Greensboro: Piedmont Press, 1965), 77, 82.

65. Stanley Hoole, ed., "Admiral on Horseback: The Diary of Brigadier General Raphael Semmes, February-May, 1865," *Alabama Review* 28 (April 1975): 140.

66. Dispatch to General Dibrell, April 14, 1865, Confederate States of America Papers, Executive Department, Special Collections Department, Duke University Library, Durham [copy courtesy of Mark Bradley, Raleigh].

67. Joseph Mullen Jr. Diary, Eleanor S. Brockenbrough Library, Museum of the Confederacy, Richmond, Virginia [copy courtesy Mark Bradley, Raleigh].

68. Zebulon B. Vance to Joseph E. Johnston, April 16, 1865, Zebulon B. Vance, Governors Letter Books, State Archives, Division of Archives and History.

69. Arnett, *Confederate Guns Were Stacked*, 83.

70. Barrett, *Sherman's March*, 258–259.

71. Barrett, *Sherman's March*, 265.

72. Fuller diary, April 16, 1865.

73. Beth G. Crabtree and James W. Patton, eds., *"Journal of a Secesh Lady": The Diary of Catherine Ann Devereux Edmondston, 1860–1866* (Raleigh: Division of Archives and History, 1979), 695 (hereafter cited as Crabtree and Patton, *Edmondston Diary*).

74. Hagood, *Memoirs of the War of Secession*, 369.

75. Hoole, "Admiral on Horseback," 141.

76. Sherman, *Memoirs*, 836.

77. David P. Conyngham, *Sherman's March Through the South* (New York: Sheldon and Company, 1865), 365.

78. Sherman, *Memoirs*, 837.

79. Sherman, *Memoirs*, 839.

80. Barrett, *Sherman's March*, 235–236.

81. Henry J. Aten, *History of the Eighty-Fifth Regiment, Illinois Volunteer Infantry* (Hiawatha, Kansas: the author, 1901), 305.

82. Joseph T. Glatthaar, *The March to the Sea and Beyond: Sherman's Troops in the Savannah and Carolinas Campaigns* (New York: New York University Press, 1985), 177.

83. Sherman, *Memoirs*, 839–840.

84. Nichols, *Story of the Great March*, 310.

85. Bromfield L. Ridley, *Battles and Sketches of the Army of Tennessee* (Mexico, Missouri: Missouri Printing, 1906; reprint, Dayton, Ohio: Press of Morningside Bookshop, 1978), 458.

86. Hagood, *Memoirs of the War of Secession*, 369.

87. Murray, *Wake*, 522.

88. Spencer, *Last Ninety Days*, 171–172.

89. Sherman, *Memoirs*, 844–845; Johnston, *Narrative*, 405–407.

90. Spencer, *Last Ninety Days*, 152–153.

91. Barrett, *Sherman's March*, 241.

92. John F. Marszalek, *Sherman: A Soldier's Passion for Order* (New York: Free Press, 1993), 349.

93. Charles W. Wills, *Army Life of an Illinois Soldier, Including a Day by Day Record of Sherman's March to the Sea: Letters and Diary of the Late Charles W. Wills, compiled and published by his sister* (Washington: Globe Printing Company, 1906), 372.

94. Thomas Ward Osborn, *The Fiery Trail: A Union Officer's Account of Sherman's Last Campaigns*, ed. Richard Harwell and Philip N. Racine (Knoxville: University of Tennessee Press, 1986), 213–214.

95. Johnston, *Narrative*, 410.

96. Ridley, *Battles and Sketches*, 459.

97. Johnston, *Narrative*, 408–409.

98. Sherman, *Memoirs*, 845.

99. Barrett, *Sherman's March*, 248.

100. *Story of the Fifty-fifth Illinois*, 430–431.

101. *Official Records . . . Armies*, ser. 1, 47, pt. 1:672.

102. Zebulon B. Vance to Joseph E. Johnston, April 20, 1865, Zebulon B. Vance, Governors Letter Books, State Archives.

103. James Sloan to Zebulon B. Vance, April 20, 1865, Zebulon B. Vance, Governors Letter Books, State Archives.

104. Crabtree and Patton, *Edmondston Diary*, 700.

105. Fuller diary, April 20, 1865.

106. Bryant, *History of the Third Regiment*, 329.

107. Denney, *Civil War Years*, 561.

108. Office of the Adjutant General, General Papers and Books, General William T. Sherman, vol. 18 (Letters Sent, April 14–July 9, 1865), National Archives, Washington, D.C. [copy courtesy Mark Bradley.]

109. Bauer, *Soldiering*, 241.

110. Jonathan Worth Papers, Southern Historical Collection, University of North Carolina Library, Chapel Hill [copy courtesy Mark Bradley]; Hamilton, *Correspondence of Jonathan Worth*, 2:1290.

111. Ridley, *Battles and Sketches*, 460.

112. Joseph E. Johnston to John Breckinridge, April 22, 1865, Zebulon B. Vance, Governors Letter Books, State Archives.

113. E. B. Long, *The Civil War Day by Day: An Almanac, 1861–1865* (Garden City, N.J.: Doubleday and Co., 1971), 681.

114. Hagood, *Memoirs of the War of Secession*, 370.

115. Sherman, *Memoirs*, 846.

116. *Official Records . . . Armies*, ser. 1, 48, pt. 3:288.

117. Sherman, *Memoirs*, 846.

118. Johnston, *Narrative*, 410–411; Sherman, *Memoirs*, 846.

119. Joseph E. Johnston to Zebulon B. Vance, April 24, 1865, Zebulon B. Vance, Governors Letter Books, State Archives.

120. Sherman, *Memoirs*, 849–850.

121. Bryant, *History of the Third Regiment*, 330.

122. *Official Records . . . Armies*, ser. 1, 48, pt. 3:627.

123. Long, *The Civil War Day by Day*, 682.

124. Johnston, *Narrative*, 412; Long, *The Civil War Day by Day*, 682–683.

125. Sherman, *Memoirs*, 852.

126. Jacob D. Cox, *The March to the Sea: Franklin and Nashville* (New York: Charles Scribner's Sons, 1882; reprint, Wilmington, N.C.: Broadfoot Publishing Company, 1989), 215–216.

127. Arbuckle, *Civil War Experiences*, 153–154.

128. Cox, *March to the Sea*, 217.

129. Arnett, *Confederate Guns Were Stacked*, 84, 90.

130. Arnett, *Confederate Guns Were Stacked*, 88, 109.

131. Arnett, *Confederate Guns Were Stacked*, 96.

132. *Official Records . . . Armies*, ser. 1, 47, pt. 1:185–186.

133. George W. Pepper, *Personal Recollections of Sherman's Campaigns in Georgia and the Carolinas* (Zanesville, Ohio: Hugh Dunne, 1866), 426–427.

134. Arnett, *Confederate Guns Were Stacked*, 112–113.

135. Ridley, *Battles and Sketches*, 464–465.

136. Hagood, *Memoirs of the War of Secession*, 371.

137. Johnston, *Narrative*, 416–417.

138. *Official Records . . . Armies*, ser. 1, 48, pt. 3:324–325. On the lines of march, see George B. Davis, Leslie J. Perry, and Joseph W. Kirkley, *The Official Military Atlas of the Civil War* (Washington, D.C.: Government Printing Office, 1891; reprint, Avenel, N.J.: Gramercy Books, 1983), plate CXVII.

139. *Official Records . . . Armies*, ser. 1, 48, pt. 3:327.

140. Johnston, *Narrative*, 417–418.

141. Sherman, *Memoirs*, 854–856.

142. Nichols, *Story of the Great March*, 320.

143. William Babcock Hazen, *A Narrative of Military Service* (Boston: Ticknor and Company, 1885), 371.

144. *Official Records . . . Armies*, ser. 1, 48, pt. 3:338–339.

145. Crabtree and Patton, *Edmondston Diary,* 706–707.

146. Ridley, *Battles and Sketches,* 466.

147. Hagood, *Memoirs of the War of Secession,* 372.

148. Sherman, *Memoirs,* 856–857.

149. Murray, *Wake,* 540.

150. Glatthaar, *March to the Sea and Beyond,* 179.

151. *Story of the Fifty-fifth Illinois,* 431–432.

152. Wills, *Army Life,* 372–373.

153. John K. Duke, *History of the Fifty-third Regiment Ohio Volunteer Infantry During the War of the Rebellion, 1861–1865* (Portsmouth, Ohio: Blade Printing Company, 1900), 196.

154. Pepper, *Personal Recollections of Sherman's Campaigns,* 435.

155. Bryant, *History of the Third Regiment,* 330.

156. Fuller diary, April 29, 1865.

157. Ridley, *Battles and Sketches,* 466.

158. Denney, *Civil War Years,* 564.

159. Cox, *March to the Sea,* 218.

160. Duke, *History of the Fifty-third Regiment,* 196.

161. Bryant, *History of the Third Regiment,* 330–331.

162. Spencer, *Last Ninety Days,* 189.

163. Bauer, *Soldiering,* 242–243.

164. Hazen, *Narrative of Military Service,* 372; George P. Metz Papers, Special Collections Department, Duke University Library; Duke, *History of the Fifty-third Regiment,* 196. The author acknowledges the assistance of Mr. Joseph Elmore of Louisburg, North Carolina, in compiling information on this segment of the march.

165. Charles Brown Tompkins Papers, Special Collections Department, Duke University Library.

166. Fuller diary, May 1, 1865.

167. *Story of the Fifty-fifth Illinois,* 432.

168. Belinda Hurmence, ed., *My Folks Don't Want Me To Talk About Slavery: Twenty-One Oral Histories of Former North Carolina Slaves* (Winston-Salem: John F. Blair, 1984), 44–49.

169. Wills, *Army Life,* 375.

170. Robert W. Winston, *It's a Far Cry* (New York: Henry Holt, 1937), 3–4.

171. *Louisburg Franklin Times,* February 25, 1938, July 9, 1943.

172. Ridley, *Battles and Sketches,* 467.

173. Pepper, *Personal Recollections of Sherman's Campaigns,* 436.

174. *Raleigh News and Observer,* August 19, 1956.

175. Fuller diary, May 2, 1865.

176. D. Augustus Dickert, *History of Kershaw's Brigade* (Newberry, S.C.: Elbert H. Aull Co., 1899; reprint, Dayton, Ohio: Press of Morningside Bookshop, 1976), 530.

177. Johnston, *Narrative,* 418–419.

178. Johnston, *Narrative,* 419–420.

179. Davis and others, *Official Military Atlas,* plate CXVII.

180. Hazen, *Narrative of Military Service,* 372.

181. *Raleigh News and Observer,* August 19, 1956.

182. Duke, *History of the Fifty-third Regiment,* 196.

183. Pepper, *Personal Recollections of Sherman's Campaigns*, 436.

184. Lizzie Wilson Montgomery, *Sketches of Old Warrenton: Traditions and Reminiscences of the Town and People Who Made It* (Raleigh: Edwards and Broughton, 1924), 252–254.

185. Spencer, *Last Ninety Days*, 185.

186. Fuller diary, May 4, 1865.

187. Duke, *History of the Fifty-third Regiment*, 197.

188. Bryant, *History of the Third Regiment*, 330–331.

189. Pepper, *Personal Recollections of Sherman's Campaigns*, 437.

190. Sherman, *Memoirs*, 866.

Bibliography

Arbuckle, John C. *Civil War Experiences of a Foot-Soldier Who Marched with Sherman.* Columbus, Ohio: the author, 1930.

Arnett, Ethel Stephens. *Confederate Guns Were Stacked, Greensboro, North Carolina.* Greensboro: Piedmont Press, 1965.

Aten, Henry J. *History of the Eighty-Fifth Regiment, Illinois Volunteer Infantry.* Hiawatha, Kan.: the author, 1901.

Bardolph, Richard. "Inconstant Rebels: Desertion of North Carolina Troops in the Civil War." *North Carolina Historical Review* 41 (April 1964): 163–189.

Barrett, John G. *The Civil War in North Carolina.* Chapel Hill: University of North Carolina Press, 1963.

————. *Sherman's March through the Carolinas.* Chapel Hill: University of North Carolina Press, 1956.

Bauer, K. Jack, ed. *Soldiering: The Civil War Diary of Rice C. Bull, 123rd New York Volunteer Infantry.* San Rafael, Calif.: Presidio Press, 1977.

Belknap, Charles E. *"Recollections of a Bummer." The War of the 'Sixties.* Edited by E. R. Hutchins. New York: Neale Publishing Company, 1912.

Boatner, Mark Mayo, III. *The Civil War Dictionary.* New York: David McKay Company, 1959.

Bryant, Edwin E. *History of the Third Regiment of Wisconsin Veteran Volunteer Infantry, 1861–1865.* Cleveland, Ohio: Arthur H. Clark Company, 1891.

Charlotte Western Democrat, March 7, 14, 21, 28, April 4, 1865.

Clark, Walter, ed. *Histories of the Several Regiments and Battalions from North Carolina in the Great War, 1861–'65.* 5 vols. Raleigh and Goldsboro: State of North Carolina, 1901.

Clark, Walter. Papers. Archives, Division of Archives and History, Raleigh.

Commager, Henry Steele, ed. *The Blue and the Gray: The Story of the Civil War as Told by Participants.* 2 vols. Indianapolis: Bobbs-Merrill, 1950.

Confederate States of America Papers. Executive Department. Special Collections Department. Duke University Library, Durham.

Conyngham, David P. *Sherman's March Through the South.* New York: Sheldon and Company, 1865.

Cox, Jacob D. *The March to the Sea: Franklin and Nashville.* New York: Charles Scribner's Sons, 1882. Reprint, Wilmington, N.C.: Broadfoot Publishing Co., 1989.

Crabtree, Beth G., and James W. Patton, eds. *"Journal of a Secesh Lady": The Diary of Catherine Ann Devereux Edmondston, 1860–1866.* Raleigh: Division of Archives and History, 1979.

Davis, E. H. *Historical Sketches of Franklin County.* Raleigh: Edwards and Broughton, 1948.

Denney, Robert E. *The Civil War Years: A Day-by-Day Chronicle of the Life of a Nation.* New York: Sterling Publishing Co., 1992.

Devereux, Margaret. *Plantation Sketches.* Cambridge, Mass: Riverside Press, 1906.

Dickert, D. Augustus. *History of Kershaw's Brigade.* Newberry, S.C.: Elbert H. Aull Co., 1899. Reprint, Dayton, Ohio: Press of Morningside Bookshop, 1976

Dodson, William Carey, and Joseph Wheeler. *Campaigns of Wheeler and His Cavalry, 1862–1865.* Atlanta: Hudgins Publishing Company, 1899.

Duke, John K. *History of the Fifty-third Regiment Ohio Volunteer Infantry During the War of the Rebellion, 1861–1865.* Portsmouth, Ohio: Blade Printing Company, 1900.

Dyer, John P. *''Fightin' Joe'' Wheeler.* Baton Rouge: Louisiana State University Press, 1941.

Eaton, Clement, ed. "Diary of an Officer in Sherman's Army Marching through the Carolinas." *Journal of Southern History* 9 (May 1943): 238–254.

Eisenschiml, Otto, and Ralph Newman. *The American Iliad: The Epic Story of the Civil War as Narrated by Eyewitnesses and Contemporaries.* Indianapolis and New York: Bobbs-Merrill, 1947.

Fayetteville Observer, March 6, 9, 1865.

Footprints in Northampton, 1741–1776–1976. [Jackson?]: Northampton County Bicentennial Committee, 1976.

Fuller, Anna L., Diary. Cecil W. Robbins Library. Louisburg College, Louisburg.

Gibson, John M. *Those 163 Days: A Southern Account of Sherman's March from Atlanta to Raleigh.* New York: Coward-McCann, 1961.

Glatthaar, Joseph T. *The March to the Sea and Beyond: Sherman's Troops in the Savannah and Carolinas Campaigns.* New York: New York University Press, 1985.

Gleason, Allan S., ed. "The Military Service and Record of Sgt. Charles H. Dickinson, 1862–1865." Manuscript in preparation. (Supplied courtesy Allan S. Gleason, Twain Harte, California.)

Hagood, Johnson. *Memoirs of the War of Secession From the Original Manuscripts of Johnson Hagood.* Columbia, S.C.: The State Company, 1910.

Hamilton, J. G. de Roulhac, ed. *The Correspondence of Jonathan Worth.* 2 vols. Raleigh: North Carolina Historical Commission, 1909.

Hamilton, J. G. de Roulhac et al., eds. *The Papers of William A. Graham.* 8 vols. Raleigh: Department [Division] of Archives and History, 1957–1992.

Hazen, William Babcock. *A Narrative of Military Service.* Boston: Ticknor and Company, 1885.

Hedley, F. Y. *Marching through Georgia: Pen-Pictures of Every-Day Life in General Sherman's Army, from the Beginning of the Atlanta Campaign until the Close of the War.* Chicago: R. R. Donnelley and Sons, 1887.

Heritage of Wayne County, North Carolina, 1982. Goldsboro: Wayne County Historical Association, c. 1982.

Hitchcock, Henry. *Marching With Sherman: Passages from the Letters and Campaign Diaries of Henry Hitchcock.* Edited by M. A. DeWolfe Howe. New Haven: Yale University Press, 1927.

Hoole, W. Stanley, ed. "Admiral on Horseback: The Diary of Brigadier General Raphael Semmes, February–May, 1865." *Alabama Review* 28 (April 1975): 129–150.

Horn, Stanley F. *The Army of the Tennessee: A Military History.* Indianapolis and New York: Bobbs-Merrill, 1941.

Huneycutt, James E., and Ida C. Huneycutt. *A History of Richmond County.* Rockingham: the authors, 1976.

Hurmence, Belinda, ed. *My Folks Don't Want Me To Talk About Slavery: Twenty-One Oral Histories of Former North Carolina Slaves.* Winston-Salem: John F. Blair, 1984.

Johnson, Bob, and Charles S. Norwood, eds. *History of Wayne County, North Carolina: A Collection of Historical Stories . . .* Goldsboro: Wayne County Historical Association, 1979.

Johnson, Robert Underwood, and Clarence Clough Buel, eds. *Battles and Leaders of the Civil War*. 4 vols. New York: Thomas Yoseloff, 1956 (originally published, New York: Century Company,1887).

Johnston, Joseph E.. *Narrative of Military Operations Directed, During the Late War Between the States*. Millwood, N.Y.: Kraus, 1981, reprint of edition published in Bloomington by Indiana University Press, 1959 (originally published, New York: D. Appleton and Company, 1874).

Jones, Katharine M. *When Sherman Came: Southern Women and the "Great March."* Indianapolis: Bobbs-Merrill, 1964.

Keys, Thomas Bland. *The Uncivil War: Union Army and Navy Excesses in the Official Records*. Biloxi, Miss.: Beauvoir Press, 1991.

Long, E. B. *The Civil War Day by Day: An Almanac, 1861–1865*. Garden City, N.J.: Doubleday and Co., 1971.

Louisburg Franklin Times, February 25, 1938, July 9, 1943.

Maclean, Clara D. "The Last Raid." *Southern Historical Society Papers* 13 (1885): 466–476.

McPherson, James M. *Battle Cry of Freedom: The Civil War Era*. New York: Oxford University Press, 1988.

Marszalek, John F. *Sherman: A Soldier's Passion for Order*. New York: Free Press, 1993.

———. "Was Sherman Really a Brute?" *Blue & Gray* 7 (December 1989): 46–48.

Medley, Mary L. *History of Anson County, North Carolina, 1750–1976*. Wadesboro: Anson County Historical Society, 1976.

Metz, George P., Papers. Special Collections Department. Duke University Library, Durham.

Montgomery, Lizzie Wilson. *Sketches of Old Warrenton: Traditions and Reminiscences of the Town and People Who Made It*. Raleigh: Edwards and Broughton, 1924.

Muller, Joseph, Jr., Diary. Eleanor S. Brockenbrough Library. The Museum of the Confederacy, Richmond, Virginia.

Murray, Elizabeth Reid. *Wake: Capital County of North Carolina*. Vol. 1. Raleigh: Capital County Publishing Company, 1983.

Nichols, George Ward. *The Story of the Great March*. New York: Harper and Brothers, 1865. Reprint, Williamston, Mass.: Corner House Publishers, 1972.

Oates, John A. *The Story of Fayetteville and the Upper Cape Fear*. Charlotte: Dowd Press, 1950.

Office of the Adjutant General, General Papers and Books, General William T. Sherman, vol. 18 (Letters Sent, April 14–July 9, 1865), National Archives, Washington, D.C.

The Official Atlas of the Civil War (New York and London: Thomas Yoseloff, 1958; reprint of Calvin D. Cowles [comp.], *Atlas to Accompany the Official Records of the Union and Confederate Armies* . . . [Washington: Government Printing Office, 1891–1895]), plate CXVII.

Olive, H. C. *The Life and Times of Rev. Johnson Olive*. Raleigh: Edwards and Broughton, 1886.

Osborn, Thomas Ward. *The Fiery Trail: A Union Officer's Account of Sherman's Last Campaigns*. Edited by Richard Harwell and Philip N. Racine. Knoxville: University of Tennessee Press, 1986.

Pepper, George W. *Personal Recollections of Sherman's Campaigns in Georgia and the Carolinas*. Zanesville, Ohio: Hugh Dunne, 1866.

Raeford News-Journal, June 20, 1930.

Raleigh Daily News, 1877, unknown date (from scrapbook collection of William Richardson, Concord, North Carolina).

Raleigh Daily Progress, March 20, 30, April 1, 6, 15, 1865.

Raleigh News and Observer, August 19, 1956.

Raleigh North Carolina Standard, March 1, 15, 1865.

Ridley, Bromfield L. *Battles and Sketches of the Army of Tennessee*. Mexico, Missouri: Missouri Printing, 1906. Reprint, Dayton, Ohio: Press of Morningside Bookshop, 1978.

Salisbury Carolina Watchman, March 7, 1865.

Sherman, William Tecumseh. *Memoirs of General W. T. Sherman*. New York: Library of America, 1990 (originally published, New York: D. Appleton and Company, 1875).

Sketches of War History, 1861–1865: Papers Read Before the Ohio Commandery of the Military Order of the Loyal Legion of the United States, 1883–1886. 5 vols. Cincinnati: Robert S. Clarke and Co., 1888.

Smith, Jessie S. "On the Battle Field of Averasboro, N.C." *Confederate Veteran* 34 (February 1926): 315–338.

Spencer, Cornelia Phillips. *The Last Ninety Days of the War in North-Carolina*. New York: Watchman Publishing Company, 1866.

The Story of the Fifty-fifth Illinois Volunteer Infantry in the Civil War, 1861–1865. Clinton, Mass.: W. J. Coulter, 1887.

Swain, David L. *Early Times in Raleigh: Addresses Delivered by the Hon. David L. Swain, LL.D. at the Dedication of Tucker Hall*. Raleigh: Walters, Hughes and Company, 1867.

Tatum, Georgia Lee. *Disloyalty in the Confederacy*. Chapel Hill: University of North Carolina Press, 1934.

Tompkins, Charles Brown, Papers. Special Collections Department. Duke University Library, Durham.

Toombs, Samuel. *Reminiscences of the War, Comprising a Detailed Account of the Experiences of the Thirteenth Regiment New Jersey Volunteers*. Orange, N.J.: n.p., 1878.

Trowbridge, J. T. *The South: A Tour of Its Battlefields and Ruined Cities, A Journey Through the Desolated States, and Talks with the People*. Hartford, Conn.: L. Stebbins, 1866.

Van Noppen, Ina W. "The Significance of Stoneman's Last Raid." *North Carolina Historical Review* 38 (January, April, July, October, 1961): 19–44, 149–172, 341–361, 500–526.

Vance, Zebulon Baird. Governors Letter Books. State Archives. Division of Archives and History, Raleigh.

Wadesboro Argus, March 30, 1865.

The War of the Rebellion: A Compilation of the Official Records of the Union and Confederate Armies. 70 vols. Washington: Government Printing Office, 1880–1901.

Wellman, Manly Wade. *Giant in Gray: A Biography of Wade Hampton of South Carolina*. New York: Charles Scribner's Sons, 1949.

Wills, Charles W. *Army Life of an Illinois Soldier, Including a Day by Day Record of Sherman's March to the Sea: Letters and Diary of the Late Charles W. Wills*. Compiled and published by his sister. Washington: Globe Printing Company, 1906.

Winston, Robert W. *It's a Far Cry*. New York: Henry Holt, 1937.

Winther, Oscar Osburn, ed. *With Sherman to the Sea: The Civil War Letters, Diaries and Reminiscences of Theodore F. Upson*. Bloomington: Indiana University Press, 1958.

Worth, Jonathan, Papers. Southern Historical Collection. University of North Carolina Library, Chapel Hill.

Yates, Richard E. "Governor Vance and the End of the War in North Carolina." *North Carolina Historical Review* 18 (October 1941): 315–338.

Yearns, W. Buck, and John G. Barrett, eds. *North Carolina Civil War Documentary*. Chapel Hill: University of North Carolina Press, 1980.

Index

86, 93; ordered to Greensboro, 58; orders burning of bridges over Roanoke River, 56, impressment, 56, troops to Bentonville, 38; plans strike on one of Sherman's columns, 35; pledges best efforts to return to North Carolina items due state from Confederate government, 92; quoted, 2, 6, 63, 68, 91, 92, 93, 98, 106–107; reacts to orders regarding foraging, 8–9; receives demand for immediate surrender, 92; rejoins his army following meeting with Jefferson Davis, 68; to replace Beauregard as commander of Confederate forces in Carolinas, 5; reports on thefts of Confederate supplies, 91; withdraws from Bentonville, 41

Jones, Robert, 76
Jones, Wesley, 75
Jones's Crossroads, 93
Jones's Spring, 97

K

Keenan, Capt. _____, 51
Kerwin, M., 49
Kilpatrick, Judson, 37, 66, 68, 69, 84, 94; commander of Union cavalry division, 1; demeanor of, described, 84; enters North Carolina, 2; establishes headquarters in Mount Olive, 48; ordered to destroy key facilities in and near Fayetteville, 19; quoted, 45
Kinston, N.C., 11, 14, 15, 18, 39, 51; occupied by Union troops, 26
Kirkland, William W., 96
Kornegay, Lemuel W.: house of, 48
Kornegay, Mrs. Lemuel W., 48

L

Last Ninety Days of the War in North-Carolina, The, 71
Laurel Hill, N.C., 9, 13, 14
Laurinburg, N.C., 15; scene of Federal raid, 12
Lee, Robert E., 8, 78, 84; quoted, 8; surrenders, 57
Lewis, Robert G., 69
Lincoln, Abraham, 6, 77, 86, 87; death of, 79; reaction to death of, 83, 84, 85
Logan, John A., 40, 57, 74, 85, 92, 96, 105; defends State Capitol against destruction by Federal stragglers, 84; Fifteenth Corps of, part of Sherman's army, 1; occupies Goldsboro residence, 43

Looting (by Confederate troops), 66, 81, 83, 89. *See also* arson; pillaging; plundering; robbery; vandalism
Looting (by Federal troops), 42, 46, 47; in Chapel Hill, 85–86, in Chatham County, 67, in and near Fayetteville, 21, 23, 25, 27, 46, in and near Goldsboro, 40; in Wake County, 75–76, 76, near Greenville, 49. *See also* arson; pillaging; plundering; robbery; vandalism
Louisburg, N.C., 79, 96, 101, 102, 103, 105, 106, 108; surrenders to Sherman, 80
Louisburg College, 105
Lowell Factory, 57
Lucas, L. T., 85
Lumber River, 12, 13, 16
Lumberton, N.C., 16–17
Lutterlough, Mr. _____, 18

M

McBride, J. G.: quoted, 7
McIver, Rachel, 50
McKimmon, Kate: quoted, 64–65, 71
McLaws, Lafayette, 56
McLean, Archibald, 19
Maclean, Clara D.: quoted, 67
McLeans Station, 89
McNeil, Rev. _____, 15
Macon, N.C., 97, 107
McPherson, James M.: quoted, 78
McVeagh, Lieut. _____(of Illinois), 21
Mallett, Charles B.: quoted, 25
Mallory, Stephen R., 63
Malone, E., 80
Manly, Charles, 73; quoted, 71–72
Marks Station (Richmond County), 12
Marszalek, John F.: quoted, 87
Maysville, N.C., 4
Metz, George P.: quoted, 103
Milburnie Mill (Wake County), 71
Millard, Bennett, Jr.: farm of, 48
Mills, 7, 10, 18, 28, 42, 45, 53, 57, 71, 77
Mitchiner, Patsy: quoted, 73
Moccasin Swamp, 57
Monroe, Charles, 17
Monroe, N.C., 2
Monroe's Crossroads (present Hoke County), 13
Montgomery, Lizzie: quoted, 107–108
Moore, Bartholomew Figures: quoted, 75
Moore, C. G. C., 55
Morale. *See* Confederate morale